Bf 110 G-2/U1 night fighter
equipped with two 300-litre drop-
tanks. (See pages 104–13.)

THE LUFTWAFFE ALBUM

Fighters and Bombers of the German Air Force 1933–1945

Joachim Dressel and Manfred Greihl

TRANSLATED BY M. J. SHIELDS, FIInfSc, MITL

BROCKHAMPTON PRESS
LONDON

Arms and Armour Press
AN IMPRINT OF THE CASSELL GROUP
Wellington Huse, 125 Strand, London WC2R 0BB

This edition published 1999 by Brockhampton Press,
a member of Hodder Headline PLC. Group

ISBN 1 86019 978X

Previously published as *Fighters of the Luftwaffe* (1993)
and *Bombers of the Luftwaffe* (1994)

British Library Cataloguing-in-Publication Data: a
catalogue record for this book is available from the British
Library

ISBN 1-85409-409-2

Designed and edited by DAG Publications Ltd.
Designed by David Gibbons; layout by Anthony A. Evans;
printed and bound in Oriental Press, Dubai, U.A.E.

Picture Credits: Part One
Arena; Balke; Bekker; Borzutski; Brieke; Brüse; Bundes-
archiv (BA); Chapman; Creek; DASA; Deutsche Lufthansa
AG; Deutsches Museum; Dornier GmbH; Dressel; DVLR;
FAG Frankfurt; Filley; Francella; Götz; Griehl; Heck;
Hefner; Heinkel Werke; Henschel Werke; Herrendorf;
Herwig; Dr Hiller; Holzmann; Junkers Werke; König; Dipl
Ing Kössler; Kudlica; Krüger; Kruse; Lange; Lutz Jr;
Marshall; MBB; Meier; Meisel; Menke; Mohr; van Mol;
MTU; Müller-Romminger; NASM; Nowarra; Adam Opel
AG; Petrick; Dr Price; Radigner; Ranson; RDAF; Rehm;
Reidiger; Reisen; Roemer; Rohrbach; Roosenboom; Royal
Air Force; Schlaug; Schliephake; Selinger, F.; P. Seng-
felder; Smith; Spork; Stapfer; Thiele; Trenkle; Wittigeyer.

Picture Credits: Part Two
G. Aders, Th. Arens (Forschungsgruppe Luftfahrt-
geschichte e.V.), U. Balke, V. Beyler, M. Boehme, E.
Creek, H. Fritz, P. Heck, D. Herwig (Deutsche Studienbüro
für Luftfahrt), K-E. Heinkel, Dr. Hiller, H.J. Nowarra, van
Mol, F. Müller-Romminger, F. Offer, P. Petrick, J.
Prowan, W. Radinger, Dipl.Ing. Ramson (ERNO/MBB),
G. Schlaug, H. Schliephake, Ph. Schreiber, F. Selinger,
Dipl.Ing. Schubert (MTU), R. Smith, H.H. Stapfer, Dr.
Wustrack, (Flughafen Frankfurt AG) and Dipl.Ing. Zucker
(Deutsches Museum München).

We must also thank Frau Monika Müller for careful
preparation of the manuscript as well as my daughter,
Nathalie Katharina Dressel, who read the text.

Part One
FIGHTERS

Notes

As German and British or American Air Force organization and ranks do not correspond exactly, the German names have been retained in the text.

Organization

During the Second World War a Luftwaffe Geschwader was roughly equivalent to an RAF Group, a Gruppe to a Wing, and a Staffel to a Squadron.

Depending on their function, these could carry a prefix such as Erprobungs- (Test-), Fernaufklärungs- (Long-Range Reconnaissance), Jagd- (Day Fighter), Kampf- (Bomber), Nachtjagd (Night-Fighter), Nahaufklärungs- (Close-Reconnaissance), Schlacht- (Close-Support), Zerstörer- (Heavy-Fighter), etc. Geschwader were referred to by abbreviations (e.g., JG - Jagdgeschwader), Gruppe within a Geschwader by a Roman numeral (e.g., I./JG 4), and Staffel by Arabic numerals (e.g., 1./JG 4).

Ranks

Luftwaffe	RAF	USAAF
Generalfeldmarschall	Marshal of the RAF	General (5-star)
Generaloberst	Air Chief Marshal	General (4-star)
General der Flieger	Air Marshal	Lieutenant General
Generalleutnant	Air Vice-Marshal	Major General
Oberst	Group Captain	Colonel
Oberstleutnant	Wing Commander	Lieutenant Colonel
Major	Squadron Leader	Major
Hauptmann	Flight Lieutenant	Captain
Oberleutnant	Flying Officer	First Lieutenant
Leutnant	Pilot Officer	Second Lieutenant

Abbreviations

Some abbreviations are used in text. Many have no special meaning, but the more important ones other than those indicated above are:

DLV	Deutscher Luftsportverband	German Air Sport League
E-Stelle	Erprobungstelle	Test Establishment
GdJ	General der Jagdflieger	General of Fighters
Jabo	Jadgbomber	Fighter-Bomber
KdE	Kommando der Erprobungstellen	Test Establishment Command
MG	Maschinengewehr	Machine-gun
MK	Motorkanone	Cannon
OKL	Oberkommando der Luftwaffe	Air Force High Command
RLM	Reichsluftfahrtsministerium	Air Ministry
RMfRuK	Reichsministerium für Rüstungskraft	War Supply Ministry
Stuka	Sturzkampfflugzeug	Dive-bomber
TLR	Technischer Luftrüstung	Technical Air Armament

Introduction

In the early 1920s a small body of officers in the 100,000-man German Reichswehr was secretly involved in building a new Luftwaffe. Felmy, Kesselring, Sperrle, Stumpf and Wever were the men of these early days. Between 1928 and 1931 many officers of the Reichswehr were trained for the future Luftwaffe at Lipetsk in Russia. However, the actual build-up of the Luftwaffe began officially with the establishment of the Air Ministry of the Reich (Reichsluftfahrt-ministerium, or RLM) on 5 May 1933. With the introduction of conscription in 1935, the Luftwaffe came out of hiding. The simultaneous announcement of military sovereignty on 16 March 1935 brought together all former civil flying units into the new Luftwaffe.

Among the best known groups was the 'Mitteldeutsche Reklamestaffel' (Central German Display Squadron) which later became the core of Jagdgeschwader (JG) 132. This led to the establishment in April 1934 of the Fighter Training School at Schleissheim near Munich, followed by others at Oldenburg and Werneuchen.

On 14 March 1935 the first fighter group was established as JG 132 at Döberitz with the famous name of 'Richthofen'. Although Junkers and Dornier had already proved the worth of monoplanes in the First World War, the fighter group was equipped initially with biplanes, namely the Arado Ar 65, Ar 85 and Heinkel He 51. New squadrons followed soon after the establishment of JG 132, and made their first public appearance during Hitler's military occupation of the Rhineland. In the Spanish Civil War, which was used as a testing ground for new weapons, the single-engined Messerschmitt Bf 109 and Heinkel He 112 monoplane fighters were tried out in action. At that time further new squadrons were being created regularly.

As a result of forming so many bomber, dive-bomber and heavy fighter squadrons, the fighter force was short of suitable officers. This later proved disastrous in terms of personnel and, because of the limitations of the offensive thinking of the German leadership, in the tactical sense. So, out of some 4,100 front-line aircraft which the Luftwaffe had on charge at the start of the Second World War, only 780 were fighters. Only after the aerial battles over Britain did the lack of superior aircraft with corresponding operational range become clear, if only because they had been almost wiped out by then. The heavy fighter groups equipped with the Messerschmitt Bf 110 were unable to fulfil expectations, and the same applied to the successor models Me 210 and Me 410. All suffered heavy losses as a result of their poor manoeuvrability compared with single-engined aircraft.

The night fighter at first led a precarious existence, since it lacked a suitable operational role. However, with the introduction of the Bf 110 C, the Junkers Ju 88 C, and the Dornier Do 217 J, it could fulfil its role rather better, so long as the Allies did not use their full force.

The first General der Jagdflieger, Adolf Galland, expounded on the theme of fighters and heavy-fighters as follows: 'If the level of fighter production of 1944 had been available in 1940 or even in 1941, the Luftwaffe would never have lost so many men on any front, and the overall course of the war would therefore have taken a decisively different direction.'

With the delivery of the Focke-Wulf Fw 190 A, as well as the equipping of night fighter squadrons with considerably more powerful aircraft such as the Bf 110 G, Ju 88 G or He 219 A, relatively well-developed systems became available to defend against an enemy continuously growing in strength. Meanwhile, the picture had changed.

Allied air superiority had forced the

Luftwaffe into an increasingly defensive role. The appearance of Spitfires and American long-range fighters such as the Thunderbolt and the Mustang (the production of which was totally unaffected by war conditions in Europe) meant that, despite the increasing quality of its aircraft, the Luftwaffe had no chance in the end. This was not changed in the least by either the first rocket and jet aircraft nor the long-nosed Fw 190 D or 'Dora'. Precision bombing of production facilities meant that, despite the immense output of 1944, fighter groups in the West, although by no means lacking in bravery, were no longer able to seize the initiative against the RAF and the USAAF. The devastating air raids on the German fuel industry, as well as attacks on the road network, meant that many units of both and day and night fighters never even reached their squadrons.

The basic error of the German Luftwaffe lay in its unchangingly offensive thinking. New dive-bomber and attack aircraft squadrons were continually being established and presented as the route to victory. The constant attrition as well as increasing Allied superiority, even with little or no fighter support, produced high losses in the crews involved. Well-trained personnel who would have been essential to the fighter force, as the Luftwaffe found itself fully on the defensive, were lost in increasing numbers. Nevertheless, between 1 September 1939 and 8 May 1945, the German fighter squadrons destroyed some 70,000 enemy aircraft. More than 100 Luftwaffe pilots claimed over 100 kills, and indeed Erich Hartmann reached 350. There was however a price to be paid: 14,300 men never returned from their missions.

From the technical point of view, the war had an immense effect on aircraft design. Aerodynamically superior fighters, culminating in the Me 262 with rocket weapons, showed the way to such machines as the American F-86 and the Soviet MiG-15.

M. Griehl and J. Dressel
Mainz/Hochheim, April 1992

Below: The Arado Ar 65E was armed with two MG 17 machine-guns and was intended for training.

The Creation of the German Fighter Force

SINGLE-ENGINED FIGHTERS

Restricted by the economic crisis at the end of the 1920s, the second Four-Year Programme of German aircraft construction between 1929 and 1932 fell well behind its predecessor. In addition to the consideration given to bomber development, four new single-seat fighters were produced up to 1932. These were the Arado Ar 64 and the Heinkel HD 43, followed by the Arado Ar 65 and the Heinkel HD 49.

The two latter types were new designs — the Ar 64 was derived from the Ar SD III, the HD 43 from the HD 38 — but they were still fabric-covered biplanes with tubular steel and wood structures. Their armament was two MG 17 machine-guns. After tests at Lipetsk, they were also equipped with racks for five or six 10kg bombs for attacking infantry. Both aircraft were powered by BMW VI engines. The Ar 65 was an undemanding easy-to-fly machine. Built in large numbers, it was the

Below: The Ar 68E biplane had two MG 17s as its fixed armament.

cornerstone of the German fighter force after Hitler came to power.

After the success of the Ar 65, the HD 43 was not followed up but developed into the HD 49 with a slender, rounded fuselage in place of the previous box structure. The desired aerodynamic effect was however offset by the poorly refined radiator, open cockpit, fixed undercarriage and unfavour-able junction between fuselage and lower wing. The anticipated increase in perform-ance was not therefore attained on the trial flight of the HD 49 in November 1932. Further development in which the undercarriage and the wing root were modified followed, and the maiden flight of the new version, renumbered Heinkel He 51, took place in the summer of 1933. After construction of the necessary production facilities by Heinkel, many more aircraft were delivered to the Luftwaffe from 1935 onwards, and the Ar 65 was discontinued.

When the Albatros firm went bankrupt, Walter Blume moved to Arado and designed both the single-seat fighters Ar 67 and Ar 68. A new development for the Ar 67 was a layout with the fin and rudder mounted ahead of the tailplane. This feature became a characteristic of all single-engined aircraft from Arado and was an almost totally safe means of getting out of spins, since it prevented the tailplane from blanketing the rudder.

The first Ar 68 was built in the summer of 1933. It was found to be extremely manoeuvrable and to have almost perfect flying qualities. Since the Junkers Jumo 210 engine was not yet available - the first test installations followed in the summer of 1934 in a Junkers W 34 - the Ar 68, like the He 51, was powered by the BMW VI. Although there was virtually no difference in the power available to both aircraft, most fighter units were allocated the Ar 68 in the 1936 equipment programme because of its better performance. This difference showed up in comparative flight trials of the Ar 68 and the He 51 by the famous First World War fighter ace and test pilot Ernst Udet at Brandenburg.

Almost parallel with the requirements for initial training aircraft came the plan for a single-seat trainer for more advanced pilots, which could also serve as a defensive fighter. Development contracts were given to Arado, Focke-Wulf, Heinkel and Henschel.

Arado and Focke-Wulf met the requirements with strut-braced high-wing monoplanes with fabric-covered fuselages. The Arado Ar 76 was convincing because of its precise straight-line flight without the least sign of yawing. The Fw 56 had an unconventional tail layout, with only a rudimentary fin and a very large rudder. Directional stability was therefore somewhat suspect. Heinkel's first proposal for a single-seat trainer was a strut-braced low-wing monoplane designed by Robert Lusser, but this was abandoned in the late summer of 1933 and

in its place Heinkel developed the He 74
biplane, which first flew in 1934. This aircraft
however had unsatisfactory flying qualities, in
particular a dangerous tendency to pitch down.

Below: Crash of an Ar 68F of JG
134 'Horst Wessel' in 1937.

in its place Heinkel developed the He 74
biplane, which first flew in 1934. This aircraft
however had unsatisfactory flying qualities, in
particular a dangerous tendency to pitch down.
There were also designs from Henschel, the Hs
121 high-wing monoplane and the Hs 125 low-
wing monoplane, but they too were not
adopted. This meant that, up to then, the
Luftwaffe had accepted no all-metal trainers.

In December 1933 the Technische Amt
LC II was given the task of drawing up
specifications for a new single-seat interceptor,
corresponding to the tactical requirements for
the 'Armed Aircraft IV'. The aircraft was to be
a low-wing monoplane with retractable
undercarriage and of all-metal construction. In
February 1934 Arado, Heinkel and Bayerische
Flugzeugwerke were given development

Left: The Ar 68H, seen here in spring 1937, differed from the Ar 68F in having a BMW 132 Da radial.

Right: Work on the runway of JG 132, with an He 51 A-1 in the foreground.

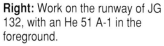

Left: The prototype Ar 68H (D-ISIX) during a flight at Speyer.

Left: The Heinkel He 51 was, with the Ar 68, the first standard fighter of the Luftwaffe. The first zero-series aircraft carried the registration D-IQEE.

Right: The He 51 B-1s of 3./JG 134 'Horst Wessel' were stationed at Werl near Dortmund in the summer of 1936.

Above: Two He 51 B-1s of I./JG 134 in July 1936.

contracts. Model tests of the Arado Ar 80 followed in July 1934, and of the Heinkel He 112 and Messerschmitt Bf 109 in October of the same year. These early trial dates were met because by the middle of 1933 all three firms presumably had projects for fighters with retractable undercarriage planned and actually waiting for the necessary order to come from the Technisch Amt. Focke-Wulf were asked to tender in September 1934 and came up with a strutbraced high-wing monoplane, the Fw 159, which had little chance against the three other designs.

For the Arado Ar 80 a special method of fuselage construction had been developed with formers and sheet aluminium panels. This structure was basically simple but too heavy and labour-intensive. Further problems arose with the undercarriage. Expensive time was taken up in various tests, so that by the time the comparative flight trials were made at the beginning of 1936, the undercarriage was fixed but streamlined. This revived the impression that aircraft should be built with fixed undercarriages. During the trials it became apparent that the Ar 80 was easy to fly, but lagged behind in terms of speed because of the fixed undercarriages. It also lost a number of fuselage panels during dives. Arado realized that this design could not compete and therefore abandoned it. However, five test models had been built, one of them a two-seater, and these were later used as test aircraft in various research projects.

Heinkel intended that the wing loading of the He 112 should not exceed 100kg/m² (this

Above right: Formation flight by nine He 51s over the Rhineland, 1936.

figure applied also for the Ar 80, although the Bf 109 had a permissible wing loading of 125 kg/m²) and therefore had to retain a two-spar wing. Heinkel also tried to use the He 70's elliptical wing form on the He 112, which was costly and time consuming to build. The fuselage was of all-metal monocoque construction with frames and stringers. Because the required Jumo 210 engine was not yet available, a Rolls-Royce Kestrel IIS was used to power the prototype. The He 112 V 1 made its maiden flight in September 1935. Flight characteristics and power were tolerable and in December 1935 it was delivered to the test centre at Rechlin.

In February-March 1936 comparative flight trials with the Bf 109 V 2 followed. In these the He 112 showed up badly in terms of power and had to be modified. The resulting He 112 V 7, with modified wings and fuselage, could finally match the Bf 109, but by this time the Bf 109 was already into its B-series, so that the Heinkel design could not catch up. In 1937 a batch of He 112 Bs powered by the Jumo 210 E engine was built and 24 of these aircraft were later delivered to Romania.

The Bf 109 was a low-wing monoplane of sheet metal monocoque construction with flush riveting, an enclosed cockpit and a retractable undercarriage. The locking mounting for the undercarriage support was located forward of the firewall, together with the forward secondary spar and the lower engine support.

The oval-section fuselage had a removable end-piece which acted as a rudder support. The two-part straight wing was of single-spar construction, had a trapezoidal planform and was fitted with automatic slats in the leading edges. All control surfaces were aerodynamically balanced and, including the landing flaps, were fabric-covered. Controls were actuated by push-rods, except for the rudder which was operated by steel cables. The landing gear was hydraulically operated. The self-sealing fuel tank was located under and behind the pilot's seat.

The Bf 109 V 1 made its maiden flight in May 1935 powered by a Rolls-Royce Kestrel engine, and in the autumn was transferred to Rechlin and later to Travemünde, where comparative flight tests were carried out. At Rechlin the Bf 109 V 1 suffered a broken undercarriage as a result of damage to the telescopic leg connections in the fuselage. This problem affected the Bf 109 right through to the end of the war, and led to high losses, especially later with inexperienced pilots. In February 1936 the Bf 109 V 2, which was powered by a Jumo 210 engine, was delivered to Travemünde and made its maiden flight on 21 January 1936. However, it crashed in April and was replaced by the Bf 109 V 3. The comparative flights in the summer proved conclusive for the Bf 109. The test (Versuch = V) models V 4 to V 6 followed, and in October 1936 underwent further testing at Rechlin.

Left: The Ar 76 was developed as a 'home defence fighter'. This photograph shows the Ar 76 V2 (D-IRAS), armed with two MG 17s.

Left: The first prototype of the 'home defence fighter' was the Ar 76a (D-ISEN).

Below: Focke-Wulf developed the Fw 56 as a trainer and escort fighter; about 1,000 of these machines were built.

Right: Most Fw 56s were powered by the Argus As 10C engine.

Right: Only three aircraft of the Fw 56 A-0 series were built.

Some of the next eight test models were powered by the DB 600 engine. At the Dübendorf Air Meeting in Switzerland in 1937, notable successes were scored against French and Czech fighters, which were however of earlier design. The Bf 109 V 13 attempted a record flight with the specially developed DB 601 Re engine and then on 11 November 1937 it reached a top speed of 611km/h.

At the end of 1936 the Bf 109 B-0/B-1 with the Jumo 210 D engine and two MG 17 machine-guns went into production at Regensburg. The Bf 109 B 2 had improved equipment and armament.

With the BF 109 C, the Jumo 210 G-1 engine was introduced. The armament was also modified to include two MG 17s in the fuselage nose and a further two in the wings. Among the equipment for the C-2 model was a test installation of an MG FFM machine-gun in the engine cowling. A few aircraft were built to this design in 1938. The Bf 109 D differed from the C-series mainly in the use of the Jumo 210 D engine. The Swiss Air Force ordered ten aircraft of this series.

Left: A camouflaged Fw 56 at the beginning of 1942.

Left: The high-wing Fw 159 fighter, here seen in its V1 version (D-IUPY), was intended to be fitted throughout with the Jumo 210 B engine.

Right: Close-up of the Fw 159's retractable undercarriage.

Far right: Nose ports for the Fw 159's two MG 17 machine-guns.

Left: Final assembly of the Fw 159 V2 (D-INGA) at Focke-Wulf's factory in Bremen.

Right: The Fw 159 V4 had a maximum speed of around 385km/h.

Above: In response to the call for Armed Aircraft IV, Arado produced the Ar 80 powered by the Jumo 210 C engine. Shown here is the V2 (D-ILOW).

Right: The Ar 80 V3 (D-IPBN) also flew with a Jumo 210 C engine.

Below: Hans Dieterle (centre) in front of his record-breaking Heinkel He 100 V8 (Works No 1905), powered by a DB 601 ReV engine.

Below right: The He 100 D-1 was powered by a 1,175hp DB 601 Aa.

Left: A typical propaganda shot of an He 100 D-1, armed with an MG FF 20mm cannon and two MG 17 machine guns.

Right: The He 112 V8 (D-IRXO) also had the DB 600 engine, which was built in series from 1934.

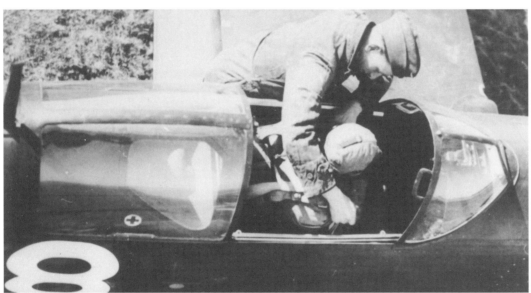

Left: Only twelve He 100 D-1s were built. They were shown to a Soviet delegation on 30 October 1939.

Left: The He 112 V7 was powered by a 1,000hp DB 600.

Right: The He 112 V12 (D-IRXS) was powered by a 12-cylinder V-engine, the DB 601, which developed 1,200hp.

Top left: The purchase of the He 112 B-0 was refused by Japan, and the aircraft was therefore offered to Spain in November 1938.

Centre left: The He 112 B-0 was introduced by the Luftwaffe in JG 132 at Fürstenwalde.

Left: The Bf 109 V4 (B-01, Works No 878) was armed with three MG 17s and flew in December 1936 in Spain

Top right: The Messerschmitt Bf 109 V3 (Works No 760) was tried out in the Spanish Civil War in 1936.

Right: No fewer than 36 German aircraft took part in the 1937 International Meeting at Dübendorf near Zürich. The picture shows Major Seidemann, Willy Messerschmitt, and Fliegerstabsing (Flight Engineer) Lucht.

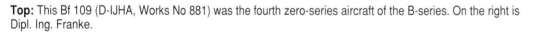

Top: This Bf 109 (D-IJHA, Works No 881) was the fourth zero-series aircraft of the B-series. On the right is Dipl. Ing. Franke.

Above: Major Seidemann climbing into the cockpit of his Bf 109 during the Dübendorf meeting, which was held from 27 July to 1 August 1937.

Below: The Bf 109 V13 (D-IPKY) was also introduced at Dübendorf.

Opposite page, top and bottom: Crash landing of a Bf 109 B-0 at Augsburg.

Above: The Bf 109 B-2 was first flown by Jagdgeschwadern JG 131, 132, 234 and 334, and was later used in several training schools.

Above centre: The Bf 109 C-1 was intended to replace the B-2 in service and was powered by a Jumo 210 Ga in-line engine.

Opposite page, top right: The Bf 109 D was first used by I./JG 131 at Jesau. Up to August 1938, about 320 Bf 109s were delivered.

Right: A total of 36 Bf 109 D-1s (coded 6.51 to 6.86) were used in the Spanish Civil War. These aircraft were powered by the Jumo 210 Da engine.

Below: This Bf 109 C-1 trainer was armed with four MG 17s.

TWIN-ENGINED FIGHTERS

The 'Armed Aircraft IV' of 1934 was planned as a single-engined fighter, from which the Bf 109 emerged, while the 'Armed Aircraft III' was intended to be a twin-engined heavy-fighter (Zerstörer). The Focke-Wulf Fw 187 was planned to be a single-seat twin-engined fighter with two MG 17 machine-guns as armament and a greater range. Kurt Tank developed the Fw 187 without an actual specification from the Air Ministry (RLM). Despite the lack of a general staff requirement, Tank approached the Head of C-Division, General Wolfram von Richthofen, in the winter

of 1935 and so convinced him of the merits of this design that he awarded Tank a contract to that specification. In January 1936 the model was produced and in December the Fw 187 V 1 was built. However, the first flight did not take place until April 1937. The Fw 187 V 2 followed in June.

Despite the advances in speed and range, the Air Ministry had no requirement for a twin-engined 'light fighter'. The Fw 187 was therefore equipped with heavier armament and a second crew member as radio-operator/navigator. As a result, the Fw 187 V 3 and V 4 models already in existence were modified to become two-seaters. The next two

Left: A twin-engined heavy-fighter of superior performance was the Focke-Wulf Fw 187 V1 (Works no 949), which was 35km/h faster than the Bf 109.

Right: The cockpit of an Fw 187, which was later armed with two MG FFs and four MG 17s.

Left: The Fw 187 V2 was armed initially with two MG 17s. During the course of testing, engine power was improved by replacing the two Jumo 210 Da engines with two Jumo 210 Gs.

Right: The Fw 187 V1 (D-AANA) reached a speed of 480km/h at sea-level.

test aircraft were also two-seaters. In addition, more powerful DB 600 engines replaced the earlier Jumo 210s in the V 6 model. Evaporative cooling was also tried on this aircraft, but due to the increased weight — from 3,850 to over 5,000kg, because of the need to carry extra water — its range was considerably reduced. In the September 1938 Quarterly Report of LC II there is a description of the Fw 187 as a two-seat fighter with heavier armament and reduced range. In flight tests in early 1939 the Fw 187 V 6 reached the (for the time) amazing speed of 635km/h at sea-level. Despite this performance, the Air Ministry gave the heavy-fighter order to Messerschmitt. Messerschmitt also won the light fighter contest with the Bf 109, although the performance of the Fw 187 was better. Only the shorter fuselage, which did not allow any rear armament, was criticized — a problem, but not an insoluble one. A pre-series of three aircraft (Fw 187 A-01 to 03) was ordered by the Air Ministry and they were tested intensively at Rechlin. In the winter of 1940 the aircraft were loaned to a fighter squadron in Norway, which reported positively. In 1942 the Fw 187 was finally accepted as a night fighter design from Focke-Wulf.

The Messerschmitt Bf 110 did not conform to the requirements of the heavy-fighter programme of 1934 and therefore formed an individual design without

Left: Crash landing of the Fw 187 V1 due to landing gear failure.

Right: Bf 110 B-0 D-AAHI which crashed near Augsburg.

Left: As the standard heavy fighter, the Messerschmitt Bf 110 acted as escort to German mid-range bombers. Seen here is an early Bf 110 B-0 with Jumo 210 Ga engines.

Right: Rear view of a Bf 110 B test prototype for the B-1 (heavy-fighter), B-2 (reconnaissance aircraft) and B-3 (trainer).

competition. Its all-metal cantilever low wing was of similar construction to that of the Bf 109. The forward armament of the third test model was increased to four MG 17s. With its two Jumo 210 engines, the Bf 110 exceeded the speed requirements of 'Armed Aircraft III'. Its ceiling however fell some 2,000 metres short, so more powerful engines were necessary. The DB 600 was not available for the Bf 110 series because of lack of development and production numbers — it was already in mass production for the Heinkel He 111.

Three test models of the Bf 110 were produced and flew in May 1936. In early 1937 construction of the pre-production Bf 110 A-0 with Jumo 210 B engines began. Its armament consisted of four fixed MG 17s in the nose and one manually operated MG 15 for rear defence. This series was later provided with heavier weapons (two MG FF guns in the lower fuselage) and Jumo 210 D engines, to become the Bf 110 B, and was released in the early part of 1938. In addition to the Bf 110 B-0/B-1, there was also the Bf 110 B-3 which was produced in small quantities as a trainer. The B-series was delivered in December 1938. Simultaneously construction began of the C-series with more powerful DB 601 A-1 engines. Immediately after the introduction of the DB 601, production of the Bf 110 in its C/D/E series commenced from the end of 1938. In the summer of 1939 the Jumo-powered Bf 110s began to be delivered to fighter squadrons of the Training and Reserve Groups as trainers.

Left: Bf 110 fuselages under construction at Augsburg.

Left: Test prototype D-AA0V in which the use of 30mm armament was tested.

Single-Engined Fighters

Right: This Bf 109 E formed part of the reserve squadron of JG 26.

Below: Test work on the Fw 190 A-1 at the Marienburg factory.

Messerschmitt
Bf 109E

The first two zero-series Bf 109 D aircraft were test beds for the new Bf 109 E series. Flight testing began in the summer of 1938 with the Bf 109 V 14 (D-IRTT) and V 15 (D-IPHR). Both machines were powered by the 1,050hp DB 601 A-1 engine. The V 14 was armed with two MG 17s in the fuselage and two MG FFs in the wing roots, but the V 15 had only the fuselage-mounted armament. At the end of 1938 a zero-series aircraft designated Bf 109 E-0 was produced for further testing. This machine was based largely on the two prototypes, but had two MG 17s in the fuselage and two in the wing roots.

At the beginning of 1939 the first Bf 109 E-1 left the production line of Messerschmitt AG at Regensburg. Only 147 E-series machines were to be built there and the majority of the 1,540 Bf 109s produced in 1939 were assembled under licence at the Gerhard Fieseler Werke at Kassel and the Erla Maschinenfabrik in Leipzig. During production

the wing-mounted MG 17 guns were replaced by the heavier MG FF 20mm cannon. In February 1939 the Bf 109 E-1 reached the Luftwaffe's fighter squadrons and was also delivered to Jagdgruppe 88 of the Condor Legion, where it replaced the Bf 109 Bs used in the Spanish Civil War. Forty Bf 109 E-1s were later sent to Spain. The Swiss Air Force purchased 80 Bf 109 Es up to April 1940, but without armament or radio.

The first effect of the opening of hostilities was the realization that the Bf 109's armament and power must be improved. In the early summer of 1939 the Bf 109 V 17 appeared, an aircraft of the E-zero series powered by the DB 601 A engine which had been intended for the Bf 109 E-3, and which could have an MG FF cannon mounted to fire through the spinner. In the autumn of the same year the Bf 109 E-3 replaced the E-1 series. During production, the cockpit canopy was improved and heavier armour for the protection

Below left: A Bf 109 E-1 of the factory defence squadron at Fieseler's Kassel factory, which existed between 16 October 1939 and 7 July 1940. In the cockpit is Anton Riediger.

Right: The early Bf 109 E-1s were gradually transferred to training establishments.

Right: A Bf 109 E-4 of the ErgSt. of JG 26 which was stationed at Rotterdam-Waalhaven.

Below: The Bf 109 E-4 was powered by the DB 601 Aa engine and armed with two MG FF cannon and two MG 17 machine-guns. The aircraft shown here belonged to III./JG 27.

Right: Feldwebel (Sergeant) Richtmann in front of a Bf 109 E of III./JG 27 in the West.

Below: A Bf 109 E-7 of 6./JG 26 in Sicily during the summer of 1941.

Right: Feldwebel (Sergeant) Richtmann in front of a Bf 109 E of III./JG 27 in the West.

of the pilot was introduced. In autumn 1940 the Bf 109 E-4 replaced the earlier model and incorporated the amended versions already in production. In the fighter-bomber version, a rack (ETC) was provided for one 250kg or four 50kg bombs, and the aircraft was given the designation Bf 109 E-4/B (the E-1/B fighter-bomber could carry only one 250kg bomb). There was also a fighter designated E-4/N with the DB 601 N engine (designed for C3 fuel), as well as the E-4/Trop with special tropical equipment. Parallel to the Bf 109 E-4, the E-5 reconnaissance version was produced with the DB 601 A engine, and with an Rb 21/18 automatic camera replacing the MG FF armament. The reconnaissance aircraft fitted with the DB 601 N engine were designated Bf 109 E-6. Also in the Bf 109 E-5 series was a special version for service in North Africa, with sand filters on the air intakes and a desert survival pack, designated E-5/Trop. In April 1940 tropicalized aircraft of the E-4 and E-5 series saw service with I./JG 27 (the 1st

Gruppe of Jagdgeschwader 27) in North Africa.

A derivative of the E-4/N was the Bf 109 E-7 long-range fighter with a 300-litre drop-tank and DB 601 N engine; it could carry one SC 250 bomb in place of the drop-tank. This too came in a tropicalized version (E-7/Trop), which also saw service with I./JG 27. The E-7/U1 and U2 fighter-bombers had a larger oil cooler and improved engine armour for use as attack aircraft. The E-7/Z version had a GM-1 nitrous oxide injection system for extra power. In the autumn of 1940 came the Bf 109 E-8, a long-range fighter powered by a DB 601 A-1, and the Bf 109 E-9 reconnaissance aircraft with a DB 601 N engine, drop-tank and fuselage-mounted Rb 50/30 automatic camera. In other respects these models conformed to the E-7 series design. A final derivative of the Bf 109 E-3 was the catapult-launched carrier fighter, the Bf 109 T, with the DB 601 N engine which was developed by Fieseler in 1939.

Opposite page, top and bottom: Bf 109 C D-IYMS was used for tests regarding the planned use on the aircraft-carrier *Graf Zeppelin*. The aircraft had an arrester hook and modifications to the undercarriage.

Above: The Bf 109 T-2 was intended to be the production version for carrier operations. It was therefore fitted with a larger wing.

Below: Most of the Bf 109 T-2s built were supplied to 11./JG 11, to I./JG 77 and to the Heligoland fighter squadron.

Messerschmitt Bf 109 F

In January 1941 the Bf 109 F with a DB 601 N engine entered production. Test models for this new series were the Bf 109 V 21 and V 24 (Works Nos 5601 - 5604). The V 21 was powered by a DB 601 A-1 engine and had all the structural improvements already incorporated in the Bf 109 F.

With this series the Bf 109 reached its most advanced aerodynamic form. The new engine cowling provided an almost ideal nose contour, enhanced by a propeller with blades that were both shorter and broader. The wing, with rounded tips and improved flaps, would be maintained in all future versions. The two flaps on the cooler outlet formed part of the landing gear cover. To improve speed even further, the high tail support and the rudder controls were moved inwards, and the tail-wheel was made fully retractable. Fuel capacity was 400 litres, and lubricating oil capacity 36 litres. Armament consisted of two MG 17 in the fuselage plus one MG FF cannon. On strength grounds, wing-root armament was discontinued, but armament could be retrofitted in wing nacelles if necessary.

The Bf 109 F-2 had one MG 151/15 in the engine cowling. When equipped for North African service, these aircraft carried the designation F-2/Trop; the Bf 109 F-2/Z was fitted with the GM-1 nitrous oxide injection system.

The DB 601 E engine became available from the beginning of 1942 and was intended to be used in the F-3 version. This series, however, remained on the drawingboard, and the Bf 109 F-4 was fitted with the DB 601 E-1 intended for its predecessor. The armament was upgraded to MG 151/20 cannon (replacing the 15mm MG 151/15), although the two MG

Below: The first Bf 109 F-1s delivered to JG 26 on the Western Front. The aircraft had an engine-mounted MG FF and two fuselage-mounted MG 17s. The engine was the DB 601 N.

Right: Close-up of the radiator of the Bf 109 F-1.

Right: This Bf 109 F-2 (Works No 9246) was tested with the Rheinmetall Borsig 2 x 4 RZ 65, a 73mm air-to-air missile.

Right: A Bf 109 F-4 of JG 54 in Russia during the winter of 1942.

Left: Servicing a Bf 109 F-4 of JG 54 on the Eastern Front. On the underside of the fuselage can be seen the attachment point for a 300-litre drop-tank (Part No R5) or one ETC 250 (Part No R6).

Right: Fitting of an engine-mounted MG 151 which projected into the cockpit of the Bf 109 G.

Left: Close-up of the 1,350hp DB 601 E 12-cylinder V engine, with a clear view of the engine-mounted cannon.

Right: An engine change in the field on the Eastern Front.

17 in the fuselage were retained. The BF 109 F-4/R1 had two nacelle-mounted MG 151/20 cannon in the wings. In the fighter-bomber version the Bf 109 F-4/B carried one 250kg bomb beneath the fuselage. Alternatively, a drop-tank with compressed air equipment could be fitted. For use in North Africa and the Med-iterranean theatre, the F-4/Trop was available. The Bf 109 F-4/Z had GM-1 injection, and aircraft for the Eastern Front had additional cold-starting equipment. The R-4 version (automatic camera) was built for reconnaissance operations. For the fighter-bomber role, the R-6 armament pack for SC 250, and drop-tank or ER 4 bomb-rack (four 50kg bombs) were installed.

The Bf 109 F was manufactured in only a single series of a little over 2,000 (16 per cent of all Bf 109s) before it was replaced by the more powerful and more heavily armed Bf 109 G. In the end, many Bf 109 Fs were used for weapons testing or in further development work on the Bf 109 series.

Messerschmitt Bf 109 G

The wartime requirement for greater power in single-seat fighters, especially after the Battle of Britain, led to the development in the early summer of 1942 of the Bf 109 G with the more powerful DB 605 A engine. With a take-off power of 1,475hp, this engine gave the 'Gustav' a speed of about 650km/h at a height of 6,000 metres. The new airframe featured a stronger undercarriage, a larger oil-tank, the previously available pressurized cockpit, provision for fitting the GM-1 nitrous oxide injection system, rear armour and head protection for the pilot, and roller-bearing-mounted slats. It could also be fitted with a bomb-rack or drop-tank.

As early as the autumn of 1941 a zero-series of several models was tested with the DB 601 E engine. The Bf 109 G-1 was conceived as a single-seat high-altitude fighter with a pressurized cabin. The aircraft went to 11./JG 1, and later a few went to 11./JG 26 as equipment for high-altitude squadrons. At the end of 1942 they first saw action in the Mediterranean.

Series production of the Bf 109 G-2 began in parallel with production of the Bf 109 G-1, and G-2 aircraft were supplied to, among others, Jagdgeschwader JG 2, 3, 5, 27, 52, 53, 54 and 77, as well as 2.(H)/Aufklärungsgruppe 14, NAG 2, and Fernaufklärungsgruppe 122 and 123. Next came the Bf 109 G-3, which was the second of the Bf 109 G series to have a pressurized cockpit. From 1943 this type was used in small numbers by high-altitude

Below: Ground staff at Augsburg. A Bf 109 G-6/R6 with 20mm MG 151/20 cannon under the wings.

Right and below centre: A Bf 109 G-5 of the home defence force with bulges covering the breeches of the engine-mounted MG 131 armament - a characteristic of this model.

Bottom right: Servicing the underwing armament of a Bf 109 G-6/R6 of II./JG 26 in Sicily.

Left and above left: In place of the two MG 151/20s, two MK 108s could be used in underwing gondolas. This photograph shows the prototype for the Bf 109 G-6/U4 series.

Above: A Bf 109 G-6 of JG 53 equipped with a 300-litre drop-tank and two WGr 21 rocket-launchers.

squadrons and by the Ergänzungsjagdgruppe West (Reserve Fighter Group West). From May 1943 fitting of the GM-1 injection system began at Antwerp.

By August 1942 the Bf 109 G-4 was being produced in considerable numbers and this version went into active service in November. The Bf 109 G-5 was the last of the series to be built as high-altitude fighters with pressurized cockpit. With the introduction of the more powerful Bf 109 G-6, the G-5 had only limited application in fighter groups. In February 1943 the Bf 109 G-6 was introduced and from then until the summer of 1944 was produced in large numbers to become a major component of national defence. The first aircraft of this series differed only slightly from the G-4, the two MG 17s mounted above the engine being replaced by MG 131s. It had not been possible to accommodate an ammunition supply within previous engine cowling designs, but from the G-6 typical bulges were incorporated for this purpose on both sides of the forward fuselage.

To improve pilot safety, the aircraft were fitted from 1943 with the so-called 'Galland Armour' with armoured glass, and, somewhat later, with the 'Erla Canopy' (the term

'Galland Canopy' is incorrect). Further modifications consisted of a partial removal of the radio aerial behind the cockpit. In the early months of 1944 an increasing number of Bf 109 G-6s had larger fins with an integrated servo-rudder.

To increase engine power at greater heights, the DB 605 AS was introduced in early 1944; this was a DB 605 A with the more powerful supercharger of the DB 603. As the engine was considerably larger, the cowling of the Bf 109 G/AS was completely modified. At the same time the ammunition supply for the MG 131 was streamlined, and a new propeller was introduced. The first of these more powerful aircraft were introduced at the beginning of 1944 in III./JG 1 and I./JG 5. Part of the older series was re-equipped to AS standard.

The G-8 series was a modification of the Bf 109 G-6 for a close reconnaissance role, and the Bf 109 G-10, which was introduced in the late summer of 1944, represented an adaptation of older aircraft to the realities of air warfare. Using various components the G-type, an approximation to the power spectrum of the Bf 109 K-4 was reached. Since the DB 605 D was not available in sufficient numbers, the DB 605

AS had to be used instead. The fuselage consisted of parts of the G-6 or K-4 series, the wing came from the Bf 109 G-2, G-14 and K-4, and the fixed armament from the G-5. The majority of the early G-10s went to Jagdgeschwader 1, 3, 4, 6, 27 and 77. In addition, these types were also found in the three Gruppen of JG 300. After production was stepped up, deliveries were made to II./NJG 11 and I./KG(J) 6. Some aircraft also went to the reconnaissance units NAG 2, 4, 14 and 15.

The Bf 109 G-10 was often used as escort and high cover for Fw 190 combat aircraft, which were increasingly being equipped with 'Panzerblitz' and 'Panzerschreck' anti-tank missiles. From the middle of 1944 some 145 Bf 109 G-2, G-3, G-4 and G-6 aircraft were rebuilt as Bf 109 G-12 two-seat trainers, mainly by Blohm und Voss.

The Bf 109 G-14 was the last model in the G-series. The first aircraft were supplied to JG 4, 76 and 77 in France in June 1944, and later to virtually all Jagdgeschwader. Among others, they were supplied as replacements to Kampfgeschwader (Jagd) I./KG(J) 6, I./KG(J) 27, and II./KG(J) 30, as well as to the first two Gruppe of KG(J) 55. Some of this type also went to NJG 11 and NAG 1, 2, 3, 4 and 14.

Summary of Bf 109 G Variants

Bf 109 G-1 Single-seat fighter with DB 505 A, pressurized cabin, Fug VIIa and Fug 25a

Bf 109 G-1/R1 Bf 109 G-1 without rear armour and bomb-rack

Bf 109 G-1/R2 Reconnaissance aircraft with Rb 50/30, 300-litre drop-tank and GM 1 injection system, without armament

Bf 109 G-1/R3 Fighter with 300 litre drop-tank (production by Erla at Leipzig)

Bf 109 G-1/R6 Fighter with nacelle-mounted armament (two MG 151/20)

Bf 109 G-2 As G-1 but without pressurized cabin and GM 1 system

Bf 109 G-2/R1 Fighter-bomber with 300 litre drop-tank and ETC 500 IXb

Bf 109 G-2/R2 Fighter-bomber with ETC 50 VIIId, no MG 151/20 cannon

Bf 109 G-2/R3 Fighter-bomber with ETC 500 IXb

Bf 109 G-2/R4 Reconnaissance aircraft with GM 1 and automatic camera

Bf 109 G-2/R6 Fighter with nacelle-mounted MG 151/20

Bf 109 G-2/U2 As G-2, but with Me P6 reversible propeller

Bf 109 G-3 As G-1, but with FuG 16Z replacing FuG VIIa

Bf 109 G-4 Reconnaissance aircraft, as G-2 but with FuG 16 replacing FuG VIIa

Bf 109 G-4/R1 ETC 500 IXb for 500kg bomb load

Bf 109 G-4/R2 Rb 50/30, no cannon

Bf 109 G-4/R3 Built-in automatic camera

Bf 109 G-4/R4 Rb 50/30, both MG 17s removed

Right: A Bf 109 G-6 with FuG 217 J-1/J-2 search radar at the Werneuchen Test Establishment.

Bf 109 G-4/R6 MG 151/20 as nacelle armament
Bf 109 G-4/R7 Radio direction finding equipment (prototype only)
Bf 109 G-5 Fighter, as G-3, but with two MG 131s replacing MG 17s
Bf 109 G-5/R1 Fighter-bomber with ETC 500 IXb
Bf 109 G-5/R2 Reconnaissance aircraft with DB 605 A-1 and GM 1 system
Bf 109 G-5/R2/AS Reconnaissance aircraft with DB 605 AS and GM 1 system
Bf 109 G-5/R3 Reconnaissance aircraft with Rb 50/30 (no series production)
Bf 109 G-5/R4 Reconnaissance aircraft with Rb 50/30, no MG 17s in fuselage
Bf 109 G-5/R6 Fighter with nacelle-mounted MG 151/20s
Bf 109 G-5/R7 Fighter with radio direction finding equipment
Bf 109 G-5/U2 High-altitude fighter with DB 605 A1 and GM 1 injection
Bf 109 G-5/U2/AS High-altitude fighter with DB 605 AS and GM 1 injection
Bf 109 G-6 As G-4, but with two MG 131s replacing MG 17s
Bf 109 G-6/R1 Fighter-bomber with ETC 500 IXb
Bf 109 G-6/R2 Fighter-bomber with MW 50 system
Bf 109 G-6/R3 Reconnaissance aircraft with Rb 75/30, 300-litre drop-tank, ETC
Bf 109 G-6/R4 Reconnaissance aircraft with Rb 50/30

Bf 109 G-6/R6 Fighter with MG 151/20 nacelle-mounted armament
Bf 109 G-6/R7 Fighter with radio direction finding equipment
Bf 109 G-6/U2 Retrofit with GM 1 system
Bf 109 G-6/U3 Retrofit with MW 50 system
Bf 109 G-6/U4 MK 108 cannon replacing MG 151/20
Bf 109 G-8 Single-seat close-reconnaissance, as G-6 but with two automatic and one Robot II cameras
Bf 109 G-8/R1 ETC 500 XIb
Bf 109 G-8/R2 Rb 50/30 automatic camera
Bf 109 G-8/R3 Two Rb 32/7x9 automatic cameras
Bf 109 G-8/R5 Two Rb 12.5/7x9 automatic cameras
Bf 109 G-8/R6 MG 151/20 nacelle-mounted armament
Bf 109 G-8/R7 Radio direction finding equipment
Bf 109 G-8/U2 GM 1 system from GM 1 base
Bf 109 G-8/U3 MW 50 system (field conversion)
Bf 109 G-10 As G-2/G-5/G-6/G-14/K-4, FT equipment of G-5
Bf 109 G-10/R1 ETC 500 XIb
Bf 109 G-10/R2 Close reconnaissance aircraft with Rb 50/30 and MW 50
Bf 109 G-10/R3 300-litre drop-tank
Bf 109 G-10/R5 Reconnaissance aircraft with Rb 12.5/7x9

Bf 109 G-10/R6 Fighter with nacelle-mounted armament and MW 50 system

Bf 109 G-10/R7 Missile-launcher (21cm BR)

Bf 109 G-10/U4 Modification with MK 108 cannon, MW 50 system

Bf 109 G-12 Two-seat trainer, DB 605 A1 engine and smaller fuel tank

Bf 109 G-14 Single-seat fighter with DB 605 A (later DB 605 AS) engine

Bf 109 G-14/R1 Fighter-bomber as Bf 109 G-10/R1

Bf 109 G-14/R2 Reconnaissance aircraft as Bf 109 G-10/R2

Bf 109 G-14/R3 Fighter as Bf 109 G-10/R3

Bf 109 G-14/R6 Fighter with MG 151/20 nacelle-mounted armament and MW 50 system

Bf 109 G-14/U4 MK 108 cannon replacing MG 151/20, MW 50 system

Bf 109 G-16 Single-seat fighter with DB 605 L engine

Left: A Bf 109 G-4 was fitted with three additional MG 151/20s for test purposes.

Left: A Bf 109 G-14AS with the so-called 'Erla Canopy', sometimes wrongly called the 'Galland Canopy', and armoured rear protection for the pilot.

Right: Ground staff at the Messerschmitt factory at Regensburg.

Right: Flugkapitän Anton Riediger was with the Bauabnahme Luft (BAL) for the Bf 109 at Messerschmitt in the winter of 1944-45.

Right: A Bf 109 G-10/AS captured by the Allies in Denmark in 1945.

Messerschmitt Bf 109 K

The initial model of the Bf 109 K was produced in the winter of 1943 at the Wiener Neustadt (WNF) factory in Austria. In addition to a more powerful engine, the Bf 109 K was notable for the use of wooden components. Other differences included improved wheel fairings and a higher retractable tail-wheel. In a GL Order of 2 March 1944 it was established that only the K-4 was to be mass-produced. The K-1 to K-3 versions with various armament and engine configurations were cancelled due to lack of capacity.

The Bf 109 K-4 was powered by a DB 605 D engine. By using a variable-pitch propeller with an electro-mechanical automatic control system, which adapted itself to changes in charge-pressure and speed, and an enlarged cooler, Messerschmitt hoped to obtain a speed increase of 20km/h. Armament consisted of two MG 131s in the fuselage and one MK 108 cannon. At the end of October 1944 the first production aircraft were delivered to III./JG 27, followed by IV. Gruppe of the same Geschwader, as well as III./JG 4 and III./JG 77.

By mid-1944 the Bf 109 K-6 with modified armament became available. This consisted of two fuselage-mounted MG 131s, one MK 108 cannon, and two wing-mounted MK 108s. At the beginning of December 1944 a model of this new 'Sturmjäger' (Storm-fighter) was tested at Regensburg. Although, according to a power calculation carried out on 11 December 1944 for the DB 605 ASCM/DCM engine, this series should have had a speed at sea-level of 608km/h, rising to 728km/h at 8,000 metres, it was never produced in quantity. However, during the closing months of the war small numbers of the K-8 reconnaissance version (with an MK 103 in place of the MK 108), the K-10 and the K-12, and the high-altitude fighter Bf 109 K-14 powered by a DB 605 L, were delivered.

Right: The test prototype Bf 109 V31 (Works No 5642, 'SG+EK') which acted as the early test model for the landing gear layout for the Me 209.

Right: side-view of the Me 209 V1 (Works No 1185, D-INJR) which was first flown by Dr. Ing. Wurster on 1 August 1938.

Left: The Bf 109 K-4 (Works No 334175) of JG 51 over East Prussia towards the end of 1944.

Right: The Me 209 V1 was produced in June 1942 and badly damaged in a crash landing on 8 September 1942.

Left: A snowed-up Bf 109 K-4 of Luftflotte Reich during the winter of 1944-45.

Bottom left: Bf 109 K-4 of JG 77.

Below: The Me 309 V1 was finally fitted with improved landing gear.

Summary of Bf 109 K-4 sub-variants

R1 ETC 500 IXb or enclosed version 503
R2 Reconnaissance aircraft as Bf 109 K-2/R2 with MW 50 injection system
R3 Enclosed 503 A-1 with 300-litre drop-tank
R4 Wing-nacelle-mounted MG 151/20
R5 Automatic camera Rb 32/7x9 or two Rb 12.5/7x9s
R6 BSK 16 movie camera built into the port wing along with the armament, GM 1 injection system

Focke-Wulf Fw 190 A

The first drawings of the Fw 190 existed as early as July 1938. They show a noticeably lower cockpit canopy which was later modified. The first flight of the unarmed Fw 190 V 1 was made on 1 June 1939. The second prototype, which retained the Focke-Wulf engine cowling and ducted spinner, flew for the first time on 31 October 1939. The Fw 190 V 3 was never completed but some of its components were used as spares for other test models. The fourth test model was broken up, and the wing of the Fw 190 V 5 was used for static testing. The zero-series began after this version.

The construction of the powerplant installation for the pre-production Fw 190 A-0 was completed by the beginning of 1940, and the series came into production at the end of that year. This aircraft was used exclusively for engine testing and, among others, the BMW 801 C/D, the Jumo 213 (from the end of 1943), and the planned 'unit powerplant' were tested. An ejection seat was tried out in Fw 190 A-0 Works No 0022 in the summer of 1943. The Fw 190 V 7 (A-0) was the test model for the main series Fw 190 A-1. This aircraft was powered by a BMW 801 C-1 engine, which was later used in the production aircraft. The A-1/U2 differed in having the more powerful BMW 801 D-2 radial engine. Four MG 17 and two MG FF were installed as armament in the series aircraft. Production of the A-2 series began in early 1942. From March 1941 the Fw 190 A-0 and A-1 were tested in action by the staff of II./JG 26 at Rechlin. Afterwards, these aircraft went to other groups of JG 26 at Le Bourget. The first air battles between the Fw 190 A-1 and the British Spitfire took place in the summer of 1941 over Dunkirk.

The Fw 190 A-2 was powered initially by the BMW 801 C-1 and later by the D-2 version of this engine. Armament consisted of two MG 17s and two MG 151/20s, plus an ETC 201

bomb-rack. In contrast to the A-1, the windscreen was made of armoured glass and armour plating was added behind the pilot's seat. Production began in August 1941 and ended in the summer of 1942. This version saw service with Jagdgeschwader JG 1, 2, 5, and 26.

Between February and mid-August 1942, the Fw 190 A-3 version was built, with armament as in the A-2 series, although the two MG FFs were mounted in the wings. In the fighter-bomber version, a fuselage-mounted bomb-rack for one 250kg or 500kg bomb, or one 300-litre drop-tank, was available; there was provision for two further 300-litre drop-tanks under the wings. As well as Jagdgeschwader JG 1, 2, 5, and 26, the first

Left: A prototype of the Focke-Wulf Fw 190 with the propeller typical of the early V1 models

Above: The Fw 190 V1 (Works No 0001) was later coded 'FO+FY'.

Below: The first Fw 190 was powered by the BMW 139 engine, although this was later replaced by the BMW 801. The aircraft shown here is in final assembly.

Bottom: The Fw 190 V5 (Works No 0015) during flight testing.

two Schlachtgeschwader were also equipped with the A-3.

Aircraft of the Fw 190 A-4 series came off the production line between June 1942 and the beginning of 1943. The most notable difference from the A-2 and A-3 series was a modified rudder with a short radio aerial. The powerplant was the BMW 801 D-2. Depending on equipment, this version could also be used as a fighter-bomber. Most of these aircraft went to Jagdgeschwader JG 1, 2, 5, 11, 26, 51, 54 and 300, as well as — with appropriate modifications — to Schlachtgeschwader SG 1 and Schnell-kampfgeschwader [High-Speed Bomber Group] SKG 10. A modified version of the Fw 190 A-4 was used as a reconnaissance aircraft and supplied to Fernaufklärungsgruppe 123 and Nahaufklärungsgruppe 13.

The Fw 190 A-5 was produced from the end of 1943. In this version, the use of the heavier BMW 801 D-2 engine meant that the centre of gravity was moved forward by some 13.5cm. Armament consisted of two fuselage-mounted MG 17s as well as two MG 151/20 and MG FF cannon in the wings. An ETC 501 bomb-rack could also be mounted under the fuselage. Radio equipment was either the FuG 16 Z or FuG 25.

From June 1943 the Fw 190 A-6 was built in large numbers and differed from the previous models mainly in having an improved wing form with MG 151/20 guns in place of the MG FFs. The fuselage-mounted armament included a further two MG 17s and an MG 151/20 was installed in each wing. During production, as well as during overhauls, a modified undercarriage fairing and FuG 16 ZE

ring aerial were installed. Most of the A-6 series were used in the defence of the Reich. To increase power, GM 1 injection equipment was tested. Some A-6s were converted to night fighters, but their performance was unsatisfactory. For the 'Wilde Sau' (Wild Boar: fighters allowed to range freely and attack bomber formations at will) Divisions, a flare-shield was installed, which made the exhaust less visible. When fitted with ETC 500 and ER4 bomb-racks, the A-6 could also be used as a fighter-bomber.

The Fw 190 A-7 was originally conceived as a high-speed reconnaissance aircraft. However, out of necessity, fighter production had to be increased rapidly, and so from the end of 1943, after the end of A-6 production, series production of the Fw 190 A-8 began. As from January 1944, the Fw 190 A-8 was given additional fuel tanks and FuG 16 ZY radio equipment, all A-8s built before that date being given the designation A-7. The offensive capability of both types was considerably increased by the replacement of the fuselage-mounted MG 17s by two MG 131s. The Fw 190 A-8 became the most important of the Fw 190 series. It differed from the early Fw 190 A-8s (later reclassified A-7s) in having a modified fuselage. The more powerful BMW 801 D radial engine was also installed. Armament consisted of two MG 131s in the fuselage and two MG 151/20s in the wing roots. It was possible to install either GM 1 injection equipment or an additional 115-litre fuel tank in the airframe. Flying weight therefore lay between 4,270 and 4,700kg. Wiring and attachment points for rocket tubes (WGr 21) were already fitted in the production aircraft. From the beginning of 1945 the Fw 190 A-8 had heavier rear armour, a domed canopy and a wooden propeller with broader blades. For fighter-bomber applications an ETC 501 was used. The Fw 190 A-9 was similar to the previous series but could be fitted with a BMW 801 TS/TH engine in place of the BMW 801 D.

In the Fw 190 A-10, a new wing and MK 103 armament were used, but otherwise it was similar to the A-9. Because of the new wing, larger landing wheels could be fitted. Also, in this last variant of the Fw 190 A series, hydraulically operated landing gear and flaps were installed. The A-10 was not a new series but basically a rebuild of earlier versions to a new standard.

Summary of equipment and armament of the Fw 190 A

Fw 190 A-1/U2 Introduction of more powerful BMW 802 D2 radial engine
Fw 190 A-2/U1 Model for course-steering apparatus and turn-and-bank indicator
Fw 190 A-2/U3 Partially armoured close-support aircraft
Fw 190 A-2/U4 close-reconnaissance with Rb 12.5/7x9 and robot camera

Left: Inspection of the Fw 190 V1 at Rechlin (left to right: Lucht, Udet, Franke), Autumn 1939.

Right: Test work on the Fw 190 A-1 at the Marienburg factory.

Left: The Fw 190 V1 was towed back to the factory in March 1940.

Right: The Fw 190 A-1's armament consisted of two MG 17s mounted above the engine and two further guns in the wing roots. Two 60-round MG FFs could be built into the mid-wing section.

Left: The Fw 190 A-0/U2 (Works No 0010) was initially powered by a BMW 801 C-0 radial engine and later with the C-1 version.

Right: Production of Fw 190 A-1 fuselages at Focke-Wulf's Bremen factory.

Fw 190 A-3/U1 Model for A-5 series
Fw 190 A-3/U2 Test aircraft for introduction of RZ 65
Fw 190 A-3/U3 (a)Model for close-reconnaissane aircraft with fuselage-mounted automatic camera (b)Model for series of six armoured close-support aircraft with fuselage-mounted bomb-rack (c)Sand filter for tropicalized version (1942)
Fw 190 A-3/U4 Reconnaissance aircraft with reduced armament (end 1942)

Fw 190 A-3/U7 Light high-altitude fighter with two MG 151/20Es in wing roots
Fw 190 A-4/U1 Fighter-bomber with a reduced armament (2 MG 151/20)
Fw 190 A-4/U3 close-support aircraft, later designated F-1
Fw 190 A-4/U8 Experimental fighter-bomber, became Fw 190 G-1
Fw 190 A-4/R1 Equipped with FuG 16 ZE
Fw 190 A-4/R6 Formation destroyer with 21cm rocket tubes

Fw 190 A-5/R1 Equipped with FuG 16 ZE

Fw 190 A-5/R6 Formation destroyer with 21cm rocket tubes

Fw 190 A-5/U1 Nacelle-mounted MK 103s

Fw 190 A-5/U2 Equipped for night operation, new designation Fw 190 G-2

Fw 190 A-5/U7 Fighter with additional MK 103s

Fw 190 A-5/U8 Fighter with BMW 801 C-2 and MW50 system

Fw 190 A-5/U9 Fighter with additional MK 108 armament

Fw 190 A-5/U10 Model for wing-mounting of MG 151/20Es

Fw 190 A-5/U11 Fighter bomber which became Fw 190 F3/R2

Fw 190 A-5/U12 Two nacelle-mounted MG 151/20s (Fw 190 A-7/R1 and A-8/R1)

Fw 190 A-5/U13 Fighter-bomber with Messerschmitt ETC, new designation Fw 190 G-3

Fw 190 A-5/U14 Torpedo-carrier

Fw 190 A-5/U15 Formerly A-5/U4

Fw 190 A-5/U16 Replacement of MG 151/20s with MK 108s

Fw 190 A-5/U17 Armoured attack aircraft, forerunner of Fw 190 F-3/R1

Fw 190 S-5 Two-seat version of Fw 190 A-5

Fw 190 A-6/R1 Heavy fighter with two Waffenbehälter WB 151

Fw 190 A-6/R2 Heavy fighter with 2 MK 108 instead of 2 MG 151 in a nacelle

Fw 190 A-6/R3 Nacelle-mounted MK 103s

Fw 190 A-6/R6 As A-5/R6, two 21cm WGr 21s replacing external MG 151/20s

Fw 190 A-7/R1 Rebuilt fighter, formerly A-5/U12

Fw 190 A-7/R2 Fighter with two wing-mounted MK 108s, later designated A8/U3.2

Fw 190 A-7/R3 One MK 103 in each nacelle

Fw 190 A-7/R6 Two WGr 21 rocket tubes

Fw 190 A-8/R1 Two nacelle-mounted MG 151/20Es

Fw 190 A-8/R2 Fighter with two wing-mounted MK 108s

Left: An early Fw 190 A-1 jacked up for undercarriage inspection.

Left: Final checks on an Fw 190 A-1 at Bremen.

Right: Tuning the engine of an Fw 190 A-1.

Right: Ground crew being introduced to an Fw 190 A-1.

Below: With its six fixed guns, the Fw 190 was a formidable fighter.

Fw 190 A-8/R3 Two nacelle-mounted MK 103s

Fw 190 A-8/R4 Two wing-mounted MG 151/20Es

Fw 190 A-8/R6 Provision for two 21cm rocket tubes

Fw 190 A-8/R7 Fw 190 A-8 with additional armour for Sturmstaffel (ramming attacks)

Fw 190 A-8/R8 Fw 190 A-8/R2 with Sturmstaffel armour (as R7)

Fw 190 A-8/R11 Powered by BMW 801 TU engine, FuG 16 ZE or FuG 125 (all-weather fighter), heated windscreen

Fw 190 A-8/R12 Heavy fighter with MG 151 armament

Fw 190 A-8/U1 Two-seat trainer with reduced armament

Fw 190 A-9/R2 Two wing-mounted MK 108s

Fw 190 A-9/R8 Attack fighter, earlier designation A-8/R8

Fw 190 A-9/R11 All-weather fighter (corresponding to A-8/R11)

Fw 190 A-9/R12 Heavy attack fighter with 2 MK 108 installed in outer wing parts, later F-8/R12

Top: An Fw 190 A-1 being refuelled at Hannover-Langenhagen.

Above: An Fw 190 A-1 showing the type of cover generally used to protect aircraft against the weather.

Top right: Jacking up an Fw 190 A-1 with hydraulic equipment; this was necessary in order to attach the drop load.

Right: Factory testing by Focke-Wulf at Hannover-Langenhagen in 1942.

Right: An Fw 190 A-1 (Works No 0047) shortly before an engine test.

Above left: Model of a robot camera installed in the wing of an Fw 190 A-2.

Above: An Fw 190 A-2 of 5./JG 26 on the Western Front.

Left: Brand-new Fw 190 fighters ready for delivery to Jagdgeschwader 26.

Left: The Fw 190 A-2 series was instantly recognizable by the cooling gills set behind the BMW 801's cowling.

Right: An Fw 190 A-3 which still has the A-1 series rudder.

Right: Changing the engine of an Fw 190 A-3 of JG 26 on 3 May 1942.

Below: The personal aircraft of the Adjutant of III./JG 26, mid-April 1942.

Below right: Most of the Fw 190 A-series could be fitted with a 300-litre drop-tank without major modification.

Above left: The Fw 190 A-6 could be identified by its four wing-mounted MG 151 cannon.

Left: To reduce the glare from exhausts, Fw 190 night fighters were fitted with flare-shields.

Below: This JG300 with FuG 218 was attached to NJG 10.

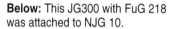

Above: Preparing for action with JG 300 in February 1944. The pilot of this Fw 190 A-6 was Oberfeldwebel Löfgen.

Above right: This Fw 190 A-8 was in service with 'Sturmstaffel' 8./JG 300.

Right: Numerous Fw 190 fighters were used as auxiliary fighter-bombers before the Fw 190 G became available.

Below: The Fw 190 A-3/U7 went into production as a high-altitude fighter after only three test aircraft.

Left: The armament of the Fw 190 A-3/U7 (Works Nos 528, 530 and 531) was reduced to only two MG 151/20 cannon on weight grounds.

Right: Front view of the Fw 190 V18 'Höhenjäger II' [High-altitude Fighter II] (Works No 0040, 'CF+OY') which was powered by a DB 603 A-1 in-line engine (Works No 17476) with a GM 1 nitrous-oxide injection system.

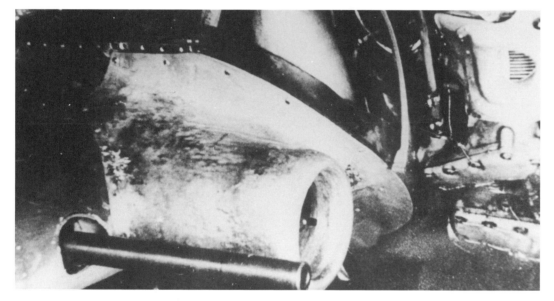

Left: Test installation of a supercharger near the wing root of an Fw 190.

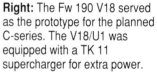

Right: The Fw 190 V18 served as the prototype for the planned C-series. The V18/U1 was equipped with a TK 11 supercharger for extra power.

Left: The Fw 190 V15 (Works No 0037, 'CF+OV') was powered by a DB 603 A-2 engine. The photograph was taken at Hannover-Langenhagen.

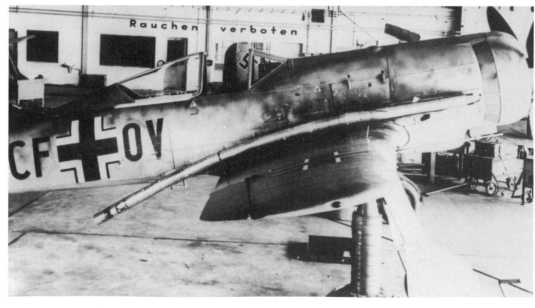

Right: This Fw 190 V18, seen in a hangar at Hannover-Langenhagen, was fitted with both FuG 7A and FuG 25A radars.

Focke-Wulf Fw 190 D

Further development of the already successful Fw 190 series began under the designations D-1 and D-2, and these were seen as replacements of all previous designs in the A-series. Production Plan LP 223 of August 1943 specified large-scale product-ion of the D-1 with the Jumo 213 A in-line engine at the rate of up to 950 aircraft per month. The first production version with the Jumo 213 A, the Fw 190 D-9, can be regarded, together with the more powerful variants (D-10 to D-15), as the peak of Fw 190 development.

One of the first models of the projected Fw 190 D-9, which had a longer nose and extended rear fuselage, was ordered in October 1942 and from the end of the year was built by Focke-Wulf. Official viewing of the model took place early in July 1943 and the order for full-scale production of a model equipped with a Jumo 213 was given in March 1944.

Prototypes for the development of the D-series were the Fw 190 V 17, V 22 and V 23, as well as the engine test versions V 53 and V 54. In October 1944 the first Fw 190 D-9 series aircraft were equipped with the Jumo 213 A-1, later replaced by a Jumo 213 C-1.

As the Fw 190 D-9 had acceptable operational safety, it became a definite part of the equipment programme. Both the Jumo 213 A-1 and C-1 were available as power units. Armament consisted at first of two MG 131 and two MG 151/20s. Two further MG 151/20s or two MK 108s could be installed in the wings, in which case the two fuselage-mounted MG 131s were removed. An ETC 501 was mounted below the fuselage as a bomb-rack or for carrying one 300-litre drop-tank. Only two examples of the Fw 190 D-10 series, fitted with the Jumo 213 C-1 and one MK 108 cannon, were produced and after tests at

Right: The Fw 190 V53 flew as the prototype for the D-9 series. In the summer of 1944 this aircraft suffered a radiator defect and had to make a forced landing at Langenhagen.

Below right: On 19 September 1944 the V53 was taken from Hannover to Tarnewitz to be tested with an engine-mounted MK 103 cannon.

Below: Prototype of the Fw 190 D with a Jumo 213 in-line engine.

Tarnewitz in the summer of 1944 they became part of the Ta 152 development programme.

The Fw 190 D-11 was the all-weather fighter version of the D-series and differed mainly in the use of the Jumo 213 F-1 engine with supercharger. According to the Factory Summary of 15 October 1944, no series production was planned. At the beginning of 1945 the head of TLR decided to begin production of the Fw 190 D-11 by the spring. The MK 108 and MG 151 armament was to remain. Up to the end of the war there were some seven Fw 190 D-11 models, the Fw 190 V 55 to V 61, of which three aircraft were rebuilt versions of the Fw 190 A-8.

Early in October 1944 the Air Ministry ordered the series production of the Fw 190 D-12 from December with the Jumo 213 E engine and MW 50 fuel injection (later, the Jumo 213 F-1 was installed), and also required the two-stage supercharger to be available, if possible, by November. Armament consisted of one central MK 108 cannon and two MG 151/20 guns in the wing roots. The Fw 190 D-12 could also serve as a torpedo launcher for the D-9 series which was coming to an end. Trials of the D-12 test model (a modified Fw 190 A-8) began in early 1945 with various types of armament. Series production began in May 1945. The Fw 190 D-13 differed from the D-11 and D-12 in having a MG 151/20 cannon in place of the MK 108; the weapons in the wing-roots were retained. Prototypes were

designated V 62 and V 71 and were converted Fw 190 A-8s.

Based on the Fw 190 D-9 was the Fw 190 D-14 high-altitude fighter with DB 603 LA engine. This variant was part of the April 1945 Forward Plan. The Fw 190 V-18/U2 and V-21/U1 were used as test aircraft. Both were then used in development of the Ta 152, especially as the series production was by now failing as the DB 605 was already intended for the Ta 152. Much the same may be said for the Fw 190 D-15, a high-altitude fighter based on the D-14, powered by a DB 603 G and armed with two MK 108s and two MG 151/20s.

Armament for Fw 190 D-9

Fighter	Two MG 131s and two MG 151/20s
Fighter	Two MG 131s, two MG 151/20s and 300-litre drop-tank
Fighter-bomber	Two MG 131s, two MG 151/20s and ETC 504
Fighter-bomber	Two Mg 131s, two MG 151/20s, ETC 504 and external 4 Schloss 50 L-2 bomb-rack

Versions of Fw 190 D-9

R 1 'Fw 190 D-9 with special armament' (two 21cm rocket launchers)
R 11 All-weather fighter corresponding to Fw 190 A-8/R11
R 14 Torpedo carrier with unit bomb-rack 504 and Schloss 301 launcher for LT IB aerial torpedo or BT 1000

Versions of Fw 190 D-12

R 1 Fighter with two MG 151/20s and one MK 108
R 5 Fighter as D-12/R1, but with PKS 12
R 11 All-weather fighter, adapted from D-12/R5
R 14 Torpedo carrier with ETZC 504 (Schloss 301), replacement for D-9/R14
R 20 Fighter with heavier armament (MK 103s in wing roots)
R 21 All-weather fighter with MW 50 injection equipment
R 22 All-weather fighter with direction-finding equipment
R 25 Equipped as D-12/R5 but with larger fuel tank

Below: The wooden propeller of the Fw 190 V53 ('DU+JC') had a diameter of 3.5m.

Right: An Fw 190 D-9 was captured by American forces near Frankfurt.

Below right: This Fw 190 D-9 served with II./JG 6 and at the beginning of 1945 was discovered by soldiers of the 69th US Infantry Division at Halle.

Above: One of the few serviceable Fw 190 D-11s available before the end of the war. Armament consisted of one MK 108 cannon and two MG 151/20s in the wing roots

Below: This Fw 190 D-11 (Works No 350158, 'VI+QM') was captured by Allied forces at Bad Wörrishofen at the end of the war.

Twin-Engined Fighters

Right: Formation flying with the heavy-fighter reserve group.

Right: Formation flight over the area between Donau and Lech.

Right: Ground crew servicing the cockpit of an Me 410 of III./ZG 76.

Messerschmitt Bf 110 C

It was not until the end of 1938 that production of the Daimler-Benz DB 601 A engine reached a rate that allowed it to be fitted to all the aircraft types for which it was intended. For this reason the Bf 110 C-0 was powered by the older DB 601 engines. In January 1939 this machine was sent to I./LG 1 for service testing. In the same month production of the Bf 110 C-1 series began. However, the monthly production rate of fifteen remained small, mainly because the 'Stuka Force' was being given priority. By the beginning of the war the Luftwaffe still had only 95 Bf 110 B-1 and C-1 aircraft, of which 82 were in serviceable condition. They were distributed between I./LG 1, I./ZG 1 and I./ZG 76. The remaining Gruppen of Zerstörergeschwader 1, 2, 26, 52 and 76 were supplied with Bf 109 C-1, D-1 and E-3 single-seat fighters. The Bf 110 B-series therefore remained in reserve and was used for training.

Even in the first weeks of the war the Bf 110 squadrons suffered heavy losses, because the heavy fighter was considerably less manoeuvrable than single-seat machines and also lacked rear defensive armament. From then on the Bf 110 was used mainly as a ground-attack aircraft or as a fighter-bomber (Bf 110 C-4/B). Employment of the Bf 110 as an escort fighter, especially in the air battles over Britain, proved disastrous.

At the end of 1941 the C-series was discontinued in favour of the Bf 110 D-2 and D-3 long-range fighter-bomber versions with underwing drop-tanks and fuselage-mounted bomb-racks. The E-series also served as a fighter-bomber and long-range reconnaissance aircraft. With the F-series, the Bf 110 was given heavier armament. The Bf 110 F-4 was used from 1942 as part of the 'Helle Nachtjagd' ('illuminated night fighter': code name for a system combining searchlights and radio-directed fighters) campaign. Produced in parallel with the F-series with DB 601 F-1 engines from mid-1942 was the better armed and more powerful G-series with DB 605 B-1s.

Summary of Bf 110 C

C-0 Zero-series; four MG 17s in nose, two MG FFs under fuselage
C-1 Escort heavy-fighter; series as C-0

Below: Factory test of a Bf 110 F-1 at Augsburg-Haunstetten.

C-2 As C-1

C-3 As C-1, gun turret with MG FF/M

C-4 Armament as C-1; heavier cockpit armour and two ETC 500/IX b; DB 600 A-1 engines

C-4/B As C-4 but with DB 601 Ns; used as dive-bomber (dive angle up to 45deg), Revi C12d sight

C-5 Reconnaissance aircraft with automatic camera; DB 601 A-1s

C-6 Heavy-fighter; armament as C-1 but with one MK 101 in ventral fairing under fuselage; DB 601 A-1s

C-7 Fighter-bomber; similar to C-4/B; DB 601 Ns

Equipment of Bf 110 C

U1 Tow-attachment for glider (C-1)

U3 Heavier armour to rear, below fuselage and around radiator

U4 Heavier armour around engines

U6 Extra armour for coolant equalizing reservoir

Top: During a belly-landing in the early summer of 1940 at Augsburg, this Bf 110 was severely damaged in both engines.

Above: Two Bf 110 Cs of the heavy-fighter reserve group in southern Germany.

Right: Formation flying with the heavy-fighter reserve group. Not all Bf 110s were fully armed.

Right: Series production of fuselages for the Bf 110 D-3.

Messerschmitt Me 210

After the annexation of the Sudetenland (Western area of Czechoslovakia) in the autumn of 1938, the Air Ministry awarded a contract to both Arado and Messerschmitt for a replacement of the Bf 110. The new heavy-fighter was to be faster and to have better armament, especially to the rear. Arado came up with the Ar 240 (limited production only) and Messerschmitt with the Me 210.

The size of the Me 210 differed only slightly from that of the Bf 110, so virtually the only performance gain that could be achieved was range, and this with additional all-up weight because of the greater fuel load. The requirement for improved defensive armament was to be met by the installation of a rotatable MG 131 machine-gun in a barbette on each side of the fuselage. The gunner had a good sideways view through a bulged Plexiglas dome, and the guns were traversed by a servo-mechanism. The crew space was wide with the fuselage nipped in sharply to the rear.

The Air Ministry had already placed its order for the Me 210 series before the maiden flight took place on 2 September 1939. However, this maiden flight showed up the problems of the Me 210. The aircraft proved to have poor longitudinal stability. This was not only disadvantageous for gun- and bomb-aiming, but also dangerous for the aircraft itself. Although this problem became apparent during the first weeks of flight trials, Messerschmitt consistently refused to deal with it by lengthening the fuselage, because this would have involved changing a whole range of components already produced. It would be a further two years before a fuselage extension and a wing rebuild would be made at the order of the Air Ministry. With these modifications, the aircraft showed acceptable flying characteristics and then, after a four-year delay, went into production as the Me 410.

Left: The first prototype Me 210 V1 (D-AABF, Works No 0001), flew for the first time on 25 September 1939, piloted by Dr. Ing. Hermann Wurster.

Lower left: Hold-ups in the development of the Me 210 occurred not only because of technical and staff shortages, but also because of the weather.

Above: Close-up of rudder of Me 210 with Works No 0026.

Above right and right: Nose section of an Me 210 used as a test-bed for the RZ 100 heavy-aircraft armament, which had a calibre of 42cm and a weight of 730kg.

Lower right: The Me 310 originated from an Me 210 A-1 (Works No 0179, 'VN+AQ'), and was flight-tested on 11 September 1943.

Messerschmitt Me 410

The adverse flying characteristics of the multi-purpose Me 210 became apparent during its flight trials. Eventually, two-and-a-half years after the first flight of the Me 210 V 1 (2 September 1939), production was stopped in January 1942. Messerschmitt then provided the Me 210 V 17 with a new rear fuselage. This modified aircraft first flew in March 1942 and showed acceptable flying characteristics. At the end of April, Göring reversed the order to end production, and allowed the Me 210 to be tested as the Me 410 with more powerful DB 603 engines and modified fuselage. In the autumn of 1942, therefore, the Me 410 V 1, a modified Me 210 A, made its first flight.

From this arose the Me 410 A-1 high-speed attack aircraft which entered production at Augsburg in January 1943. The two-seat Me 410 was powered by two DB 603 A-1 engines with provision for the GM 1 nitrous oxide injection system, which gave it a maximum speed of 615km/h. Flying weight was 11,240kg, of which 1,000kg was internal bomb-load.

The Me 410 A-1/U1 reconnaissance version had a camera mounted vertically in the centre of the fuselage. The A-1/U2 heavy-fighter version was equipped with two extra MG 151/20s mounted in the bomb bay using a special WB 151 'weapons container'. From the beginning of 1944, another reconnaissance version, the Me 410 A-3, became available to the long-range reconnaissance squadrons. This

Below: The fixed armament of Me 410 B-2/U2/R5 was four MG 151/20s, which were mounted in the former bomb bay.

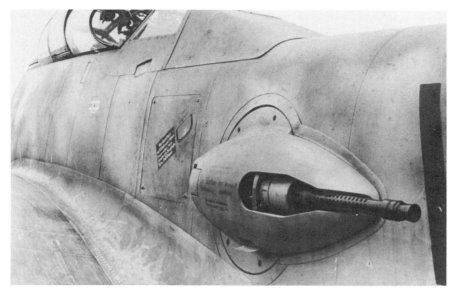

was fitted with two Rb 75/30 automatic cameras and MG 17 armament.

By that time the Me 410 A-1 was also being mass-produced by Dornier. In April 1944, production of the Me 410 B-1 was transferred entirely from Messerschmitt to Dornier. This high-speed bomber differed from the A-series in having more powerful DB 603 G engines of 1,900hp each. As with the A-series, there was also a reconnaissance version, the Me 410 B-3. The Me 410 B-2 was a heavy-fighter version. From early 1944, some Me 410 B-6s equipped with FuG 200 search radar were used against naval forces from Lorient in France. In these aircraft both MG 17s were replaced by MG 131s. In addition, they received as standard equipment the WB 103 with two MK 103 cannon. The Me 410 B-5 torpedo-carrying version did not get beyond the flight-testing stage.

In September 1944 production of the Me 410 was stopped because of the need to produce fighters. Even before that the Me 410 was reverting to the heavy-fighter duties rather than the high-speed bomber role it had played hitherto. The reconnaissance version remained in service. In all, some 1,160 Me 410s were produced by Messerschmitt at Regensburg and Augsburg, and by Dornier at Oberpfaffenhofen.

Top: Close-up of the FDSL remote-controlled barbette, fitted with an MG 131. The gunsight is clearly visible through the rear glazed section of the cockpit.

Above: Two Me 410 heavy-fighters of ZG 76 at Königsberg in 1944.

Right: An Me 410 B of III.Gruppe of ZG 76 jacked up on the weapons range.

Right: The remains of a damaged Me 410 B-1 shortly before the end of the war.

Dornier
Do 335

The development of the Do 335 arose from the High-Speed Bomber Requirement of 28 September 1942. In mid-January 1943 the Air Ministry awarded Dornier with a contract and on 18 April the official model inspection took place. The twin-engined high-speed bomber first flew on 26 October 1943 at Oberpfaffenhofen with Flugkapitän Hans Dieterle at the controls.

The role of the Do 335 varied frequently during the next few years. In November 1943 the development programme was aimed chiefly at producing a high-speed bomber rather than the heavy fighter, night fighter or reconnaissance versions. In January 1944 this priority was changed. Then the reconnaissance version was given priority over the heavy fighter, followed by the high-speed bomber

and night fighter. In this respect, the requirements of the General der Kampfflieger (Bomber Force) were diametrically opposed to those of the General der Jagdflieger (Fighter Force). At the end of March 1944 came the order to hold back the bomber versions and accelerate production of the heavy fighter. Only three months later the Do 335 A-1 and A-2 versions were delivered as bomber aircraft. From the beginning of August 1944, the Do 335 A-6 night fighter was given priority over the Do 335 A-3 reconnaissance aircraft. Again, after only two months up to 26 September 1944, development of the night fighter was postponed and emphasis was once more given to the heavy-fighter version. On 10 October the Luftwaffe leadership changed its opinion yet again and ordered a new series of night

Left: Close-up of the DB 603 A-1 engine fitted to a Dornier Do 335 A-0.

Above: Fitting the rear DB 603 A engine to a Do 335 A-1.

Below: The prototype Do 335 V-13 heavy-fighter ('RP+UA'), produced to the Building Requirement of 31 May 1944, with two additional MK 103s.

fighters. The next month, on 15 November, the prototype for the night fighter version, the Do 335 A-6, became available.

The basic tests of the Do 335 were carried out with two prototypes and two A-0 series aircraft at Rechlin. Up to the end of February 1945 only unsatisfactory results had been

achieved: the Do 335 could not reach its design performance at 7,800 metres. The type was equipped with an ejection seat and nose wheel undercarriage. It was produced in fourteen test models and a pre-series of ten Do 335 A-0 aircraft. There then followed a few Do 335 A-1 fighter-bombers, and some more two-seaters

with dual control; the latter had tandem seats for training purposes. Then came a study project for a night fighter. The long-range reconnaissance version Do 335 A-4, planned in the autumn of 1944, was never produced.

At the end of 1945 the Do 335 was discontinued in favour of the Focke-Wulf Ta 152. The explanation was that, up to the beginning of production of the series in May 1944, the Do 335 was considerably more powerful than any enemy aircraft. But only a year later after experience in action it was evident that this superiority had been considerably reduced, especially in the night fighter version. As a day heavy-fighter, the Do 335 had a small speed advantage over the Ta 152, but was no better in terms of range or endurance. Fuel consumption was also too great, and production and repair costs too high.

Left: A two-seat trainer similar to the Do 335 A-10 (Works No 240112) shown here was converted to an auxiliary night fighter.

Left: The Do 335 V-17, a two-seat night fighter, was completed at Mengen/Württ at the beginning of 1947 (!) and flew for the first time on 2 April 1947.

High-Altitude Fighters

Right: The Ta 152 H-0 (Works No 0003) at Langenhagen. With the MW 50 methanol-water injection system the power of the Jumo 213 E-1 engine was boosted to a maximum of 2,050hp.

Below: Model tests of the Me 109 H with extended wings.

Messerschmitt Bf 109 H

In early 1942 Messerschmitt received an order to design a high-altitude fighter in addition to a single-seat fighter for aircraft-carrier service. Because of the heavy workload in the design and production divisions, the construction of two special aircraft was practically impossible, so to hasten development of the proposed carrier version, a Bf 109 G with increased wing area and a stronger undercarriage was selected. At the same time Messerschmitt improved the armament by adding two MG 151s in the wing roots. As an extension to its application, it inevitably became part of the high-altitude fighter project, by exchanging the DB 605 engine for a DB 628 and adding extended wing tips, without a great deal of further development work. With a ceiling of 14,000m, it met the requirement. The aircraft was first given the designation Me 155. Work on this project was carried out in Paris and development took place extremely slowly.

In January 1943 the aircraft-carrier programme was cancelled and with it the application of the Me 155 as a carrier-based aircraft. The high-altitude version based on the Me 155 was passed on to Blohm und Voss for

further development and Messerschmitt now turned to the Me 209.

On 23 April 1943 Messerschmitt received an order from the Air Ministry for the 'Me 209 High-Altitude Fighter with DB 628'. The performance of this machine was almost identical with that of the Me 155 high-altitude fighter. However, Messerschmitt received only a verbal order to investigate whether a greater ceiling than 14,000m was feasible. From calculations carried out under this order arose the project P 1091 'Extreme High-Altitude Fighter', with a theoretical ceiling of 17,500m. This was intended to be powered by a DB 603 A with a TK 15 supercharger and a six-bladed airscrew of 4.0m diameter. Armament was to be one MK 108 cannon and two MG 151s or two MK 108s. An initial weight of 6,000kg was envisaged. A second variant was to be powered by a DB 605 A with a 3.4m-diameter airscrew. The airframe was to be that of the Me 109 extended by 2m. The remaining data corresponded to the first P 1091 project.

Since forward planning showed that series production of these machines could not be expected before the end of 1944, it was decided to produce an 'Early-Availability

Left: Model tests of the Me 109 H with extended wings.

High-Altitude Fighter' by modifying an existing model. This aircraft was expected by the Air Ministry to have a ceiling of between 13,000 and 15,000m, and was designated Bf 109 H. The intention was to build a first batch of 200 aircraft and thereafter reach a production rate of 20 to 30 machines per month. The Bf 109 H was intended primarily as an interceptor for use against enemy high-altitude reconnaissance aircraft; a plan to use it as a high-altitude fighter-bomber was abandoned on static grounds. To save weight, the rear armour was removed, only the armoured windscreen being retained. Fuselage construction was similar to that of the Bf 109 G-6, but with a pressurized cockpit. The mass-produced wing was extended by the addition of a rectangular centre-section and new tips, increasing the wingspan from 9.92m to 13.25m and wing area from 16.05m^2 to 21,90m^2. The main landing gear was also modified and, after a few flights, its track widened. The tail-wheel assembly was lengthened by 0.30 m and was non-retractable, and the landing gear fairings were removed.

The first aircraft, Bf 109 V 54 (Works No 15708, coded 'PV+JB') flew a mere ten weeks after construction began, on 5 November 1943, at Augsburg with test pilot Fritz Wendel at the controls. Further test flights followed up to 22 January 1944 with test pilots Baur, Schmidt and Lukas. The flying qualities were first described as satisfactory, with straight-line stability; pitch-down or breakout on take-off and landing were reported as very good. The second V-model, the V 55, was used as a power augmentation test-bed, and its airframe also received various aerodynamic improvements. However, this second and last serviceable machine was totally destroyed in an air raid on 25 February 1944. Attempts were then made to bring the first test model up to the standard of the V 55, but this proved impossible due to falling capacity and the commencement of production of the Me 262 jet fighter.

In early 1944 Oberstlt Kneemeyer test-flew the Bf 109 V 54 at Rechlin. He concluded that the flying characteristics of the Bf 109 H in all three axes ranged from satisfactory to particularly bad. This was confirmed by Dipl-Ing Beauvais. Despite the miserable flying characteristics, plans to put the H-series into production were almost complete. Jigs made in Italy were ready by 15 July 1944 and had been delivered to WNF (Wiener-Neustädter Flugzeugwerke GmbH) by November. They were intended for the production of the Bf 109 H-2, H-2/R-2 and H-3 variants.

At the Oberbayerische Forschungsanstalt (Research Establishment) at Oberammergau as late as November 1944, Messerschmitt was planning a third experi-mental aircraft in addition to the Bf 109 H V 54 and V 55. However, the Air Ministry cancelled the Bf 109 H on 18 July 1944 in favour of the Me 262 A-1a/U3 reconnaissance aircraft. The remaining Me 109 V 54 was presumably destroyed in the bombing raid on the Daimler-Benz Stuttgart plant on 14 August 1944.

Focke-Wulf Ta 152 H

The remarkable Allied development of high-altitude bombers with pressurized cockpits caused Germany to develop improved high-altitude fighters. Focke-Wulf received an order similar to that given to Messerschmitt, and Kurt Tank, their famous Chief Designer, produced a design for high-altitude and escort fighters with Jumo 213 in-line engines based on the Fw 190 A. By the beginning of 1942 tests with an Fw 190 were carried out and at the end of September the first Fw 190 with a Jumo 213 A in-line engine flew as the predecessor to the Ta 153 (design with DB-engine). In April 1943 further flight testing took place at the test centre. After correspondence in August 1943, some simplification and alterations were made, and the type number was changed to Ta 152.

At the beginning of 1944 work started on the first prototype of the Ta 152 H-0 series but was delayed due to staff problems. In March 1944 the factory foundations were laid at Sorau. At the same time an unprotected fuel tank was incorporated in the wing — to increase range, which entailed some redesign of the wing.

The first flight of the Ta 152 H escort version was made on 6 August 1944, but the aircraft was damaged in an emergency landing. Two weeks later the second test aircraft flew, but this crashed on 24 August after engine trouble. At the end of September the third prototype flew, and in the middle of December the first production model — however, not the

Below: The Ta 152 V6 (Works No 110006, 'VH+EY'), a forerunner of the C-0 series, was tested at Langenhagen between December 1944 and January 1945.

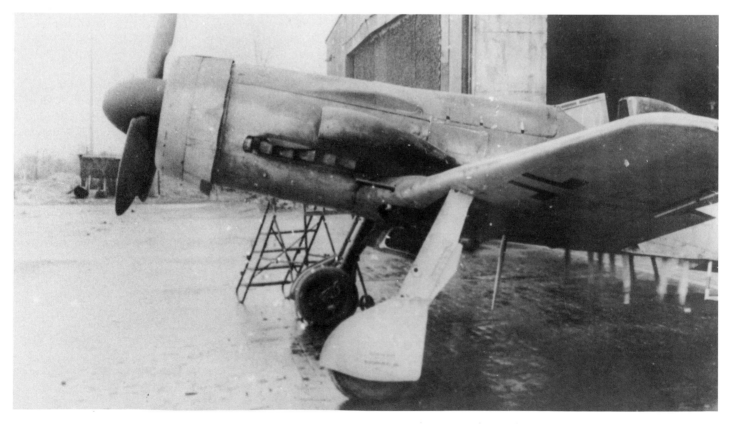

Above: Close-up of the Jumo 213 E-1 engine mounted in a Ta 152. At sea-level this engine developed 1,750hp, falling to 1,320hp at 11,000m altitude.

final design (H-0) — arrived at the test establishment. In January 1945 three standard aircraft ('Normaljäger') were ready for flying, although with the DB 603 E engine since the DB 603 L was still not ready for production. At the Sorau factory, 26 further standard aircraft were produced and divided into the various H versions. Aircraft of the H-0 series were powered by Jumo 213 E engines. They had an extended and strengthened fuselage, a pressurized cockpit, an engine-mounted MK 108 30mm cannon, and two MG 151 20mm cannon in the wing roots.

The Ta 152 V 5 and the Fw 190 V18/U 2 were the prototypes for the series of Ta 152 H-1 escort fighters produced by the Focke-Wulf factory at Cottbus from the middle of January 1945, and from March 1945 at the Erla and Gotha factories. Production aircraft had a new wing with six additional tanks, a GM-1 nitrous oxide injection system installed in the fuselage and an MW methanol-water injection system fitted in the wing; each could be used independently at altitude.

Summary of Ta 152 Series

Ta 152 C-1 and **C-3** Standard fighter with one MK 108 cannon and four MG 151/20s, or one MK 103 and four KG 151/15s; Daimler-Benz DB 603 L engine

Ta 152 B-5 Heavy-fighter with Jumo 213 E engine and three MK 103 cannon

Ta 152 H-1 Escort fighter with one MK 108 cannon and two MG 151/20s, pressurized cockpit, GM-1 injection equipment and Jumo 213 E engine

Ta 152 E Reconnaissance-fighter with armament as in the Ta 152 H-1, photographic equipment as standard in fuselage, derived from standard fighter; Jumo 213 E in-line engine

Ta 152 H-10 Escort reconnaissance aircraft with armament as Ta 152 H-1, photographic equipment as standard in fuselage, derived from escort fighter; Jumo 213 E engine

Ta 152 equipment

R 1 Camera-mount for reconnaissance (installed in E-1 and H-10)
R 11 LGW K23 navigation equipment
R 21 MW 50 high-pressure injection equipment in the wings, PKS 12 and FuG 152
R 31 GM-1 equipment with compressed air and 10.5kg trim weight (H-1)

Focke-Wulf Fw 190 B/C

By the middle of 1942 the Luftwaffe's front-line squadrons had already been supplied with an improved high-altitude aircraft, the Fw 190 A. From the autumn of that year, Focke-Wulf made great efforts to increase the aircraft's ceiling. This began with tests on pressurized cockpits and on the GM 1 nitrous oxide fuel injection system. The next stage was to test an Fw 190 B fitted with a BMW 801 TJ engine with exhaust-gas supercharger, and having a pressurized cockpit and increased wing area. A second series of prototypes intended for the DB 603 engine was designated Fw 190 C. A test series produced with the Jumo 213 in-line engine marked the beginning of the D-series. Work on all three models commenced in early 1943.

For tests on the pressurized cockpit, Focke-Wulf fell back on three Fw 190 A-3/U7 models. The flight tests revealed many problems in sealing the cockpit. From early 1943 the B-0 series began tests at Rechlin. The next two aircraft, a fourth B-0 and a B-1, also had pressurized cockpits and, for the first time, the GM 1 injection system. In April 1944 the Fw 190 B-0 went over to BMW. The B-1 series included the Fw 190 V 45 and V 47 test aircraft with GM 1 injected BMW 801 D engines but without pressurized cockpits.

The first machines of the C-series (V 13, V 15 and V 16) were mainly test aircraft for the high-altitude DB 603 engine, without pressurized cockpits. From the end of 1942 the Fw 190 V 18 became the model for the planned high-altitude fighter series with a TK-11 supercharger and DB 603 engine, although still lacking a pressurized cockpit. The TK 11 was installed under the fuselage. From 10 December 1942 the V 18/U1, designated 'Känguruh' (Kangaroo), went for tests to Daimler-Benz.

From March 1943 Fw 190s V 29 to V 33 with the TK-11 turbocharged DB 603 S engine followed, this time with pressurized cockpits. Some of these aircraft of the C-series were later modified as Ta 152 Hs. Since the BMW 801 TJ and DB 603 engines were not yet in full production, both the Fw 190 D and the Ta 152 versions finally flew with Jumo 213 engines.

Night Fighters

Above: Two Do 215 B-5 night fighters of 5./NJG 5 during a formation flight. The aircraft in the background has an two additional 20mm cannon fitted below the forward fuselage.

Right: A Ju 88 G-1 of NJG 3 which was based at Grove in 1945.

Dornier Do 17, 215, 217 J/N

The development of the Dornier night fighters proceeded initially in three stages: the Do 17 Z-7 as test prototype; the Do 17 Z-10 as production aircraft; and the Do 215 B-5 with DB 601 in-line engine. The first and, presumably only, Do 17 Z-7 was tested by I./NJG 2, and in fact it was in this aircraft that Oberleutnant Streib shot down an RAF Whitley bomber on 20 July 1940. However, only a small batch of Do 17 Z-10s was built, with nose armament consisting of one MG 151 and four MG 17s. Most went to

I./NJG 2 which had up to seven of these aircraft in service. A Do 17 Z-10 coded 'CD+PV' was used to test the FuG 212 Lichtenstein radar at Werneuchen. With the appearance of improved night fighters however, the Do 17 Z-10 came to the end of its useful life.

The next stage was the development of the Do 215 B from the Do 17 Z, and several of these machines were equipped with the nose armament of the Do 17 Z-10. A successful night attack was carried out by Oberleutnant

Below: This Do 17 Z-10 was used for testing the Spanner night-sight.

Becker in Do 215 B-5 'G9+OM' on the night of 8/9 August 1941 using the new FuG 202 B/C. Some of the Do 215 B-5s flew with II./NJG 1 and 14./NJG 1 in early 1943. Several Do 215 night fighters were equipped with the 'Spanner' night-sight which was built into the windscreen.

In October 1940 some Do 217 E bombers were converted to night fighters and were powered by either the BMW 801 radials or DB 603 in-line engines and were designated Do 217 J and Do 217 N respectively. Production of the J-1 began in March 1941. Peak production levels were reached in May 1942 but production fell off rapidly thereafter, when the Air Ministry chose the Junkers Ju 88 C-6, after which the Do 217 N was first tested in November 1942. The prototypes were the Do 217 N-01 to N-03 ('GG+YA' to 'GG+YC'), which had been equipped with four MG FFs in place of MG 151/20s. The first aircraft without the C-Stand bomb rack was designated Do 217 N-1/U-1. Defensive armament was removed from the N-2 and eventually all unnecessary equipment was deleted.

Following a proposal from Hauptmann Schoenerts, the Do 217 was equipped with upward-firing guns, set at an oblique angle. In July 1942 three Do 217 Js were armed in this way with four MG 151/20s and tests with these were carried out by 3./NJG 3. The first Do 217 N-2 ('PE+AW') had however already been equipped with improved upward-firing armament, with MG 151/20s, in addition to the standard nose guns. Up to the end of 1943, 157 of these Do 217 night fighters, mainly of J-1 and J-2 types (with Lichtenstein radar) were produced. In early 1943 the Do 217 Ns powered by DB 603 engines were progressively replaced. After about 340 Do 217 night fighters had been built the series was discontinued.

The first Do 217 J-1s, still without radar, entered service as super-heavy night fighters with 4./NJG 1 in 1942. Later, 8./NJG 2, 3./NJG 3, and 6./NJG 4 were equipped with Dornier night fighters. In addition to engine problems, their flying characteristics left something to be desired and the landing gear proved to be source of weakness. However, the Do 217 was more successful as a bomber. Difficulties with the delivery of engines and technical problems with the DB 603 meant that many of the Dornier airframes were useless and had to be scrapped.

In October 1943 many Do 217 night fighters were concentrated in Geschwadern 4, 100 and Schulgeschwader (Training Group) 101, to improve the supply of spare parts. Some of the aircraft were given to Luftwaffe communications squadrons. Other night fighters had their deficient DB 603 engines replaced by the less powerful BMW 801s and were sent to training groups such as Schulgruppe IV./NJG 101 in Hungary. Apart from the units mentioned above, Do 217 J and N aircraft also saw service with Stab IV./NJG 2, with 4. and 5./NJG 3, 11./NJG 4, Stab NJG 100, with 9.,11.,14. and 18./NJG 101, and finally with 18./NJG 200.

Above left: The Do 17 Z-10 was usually armed with one MG FF and four MG 17s. In addition to the Spanner night-sight, it also had a searchlight.

Above: Personnel of II./NJG 2 in front of a Do 215 B-5 in May 1942.

Left: A Do 217 J-1 with FuG 202 radar, the weight of which made the aircraft too slow.

Right: This Do 217 J-1, photographed in 1942 in southern Germany, was attached to a reserve unit.

Left: The zero-series aircraft of the Do 217 N-1 was designed as a heavy night fighter. Tests took place at Rechlin up to 1943.

Right: The Do 217 N-04 (Works No 1404, 'GG+YD') had eight nose-mounted guns, plus two MG 131s for defence.

Right: Feldwebel Kustusch's Do 217 N-1 of III./NJG 6 after a forced landing in Hungary.

Left: The seventh zero-series aircraft ('GG+YG') was powered by two DB 603 A-1/A-2 in-line engines and was very heavily armed.

Right: Clearly visible on this crashed Do 217 of NJG 6 is the flare-shield on the side of the DB 603 A-1 engine.

Junkers Ju 88 C/R

Soon after the first studies for the conversion of the Ju 88 A-1 bomber to a heavy-fighter with Jumo 211 B engines, the C-1 to C-5 designs appeared. There was only a single Ju 88 C-1, followed by the C-2 with its five-gun armament. The Ju 88 C-4 corresponded to the C-2 but had two Jumo 211 F engines. The C-5 flew as a heavy fighter with BMW 801 radials. The widely used Ju 88 C-6 was a replacement for the Ju 88 A-5, which had first been planned to have a 'Waffentropfen' bomb rack rather than the C-Stand. The first night fighters had some all-weather capability although they did not all have suitable radar. However, their extensive operational range allowed them to be successful night intruders on long-range operations over Britain and North Africa.

The first prototype of a Ju 88 C with Lichtenstein radar was produced in March 1943 and re-equipped shortly afterwards. At the same time the creation of the Ju 88 C-6 was considered, since the supply of Bf 110 night fighters was not sufficient to meet demand. General Kammhuber regarded the Ju 88 C-6 as obsolete and demanded rapid replacement with

Left: The Junkers Ju 88 V19 (Works No 0373), which was also designated Ju 88 Z19, was tested with additional 20mm armament.

Above: A Ju 88 C-2 of IV./KG 40 at Bordeaux-Mérignac.

Right: The SG 212 aiming apparatus intended for use with the FuG 212 Lichtenstein radar of a Ju 88 C-6.

the Ju 88 G-1. Despite a bottleneck at the BMW engine works lasting for several months, the series was finally fitted with the desired powerplant. From September 1943 Ju 88 C night fighters were equipped with the SN-2 search radar, and the call for more power was finally heard.

In 1942 Generalfeldmarschall Milch had ordered that the Ju 88 C-6 be powered by BMW 801s with GM-1 injection, but this proved impossible because of the inadequate engines. In March 1943 therefore, after several

prototypes, the Ju 88 R-series came into existence. Tests were also carried out on a Ju 88 C-6 with two Jumo 213 engines, which increased speed by 90km/h. However, as this engine was not available in sufficient numbers, it could not be used in service. Similar considerations applied to plans to fit the Ju 88 C-6 with the TK 11 supercharger. These high-altitude fighters remained on the drawing-board.

At the end of 1943 the Ju 88 R-1 and R-2 series entered production. Powered by two

Left: The cramped cockpit of the Ju 88 C heavy-fighter and night fighter can be seen in these two photographs. Note the armament which intruded into the cockpit.

Below: The Ju 88 C-5, a two-seat heavy-fighter with BMW 801 A engines, was only built as a test model.

BMW 801 engines, they also differed slightly in radio equipment and powerplant details. The Ju 88 R-2 series was fitted with SN-2 radar. Some aircraft had upward-firing armament similar to that of the Ju 88 C, consisting of two MG 151/20s. In August 1944 the Ju 88 C-6 and R-2 were still being mass-produced in addition to the Ju 88 G. Night fighters of the C and R series were supplied to virtually all night fighter groups. Both series were finally superseded by the Ju 88 G-1 and G-6. Remaining aircraft were recalled and sent to training squadrons.

Junkers Ju 88 G

As early as February 1942 plans were in existence for the production of 100 Ju 88 G night fighters. In May 1943 the requirement went up to 700 and in 1944 to more than 1800. On 26 October 1943 it became abundantly clear that, just as with the Ju 88 R-2, there would be problems in obtaining engines for the Ju 88 G, in terms of numbers as well as scheduling.

The first G-series aircraft had the nose section of the Ju 88 A-4, the fuselage of the Ju 188 E-1, the wings of the Ju 88 D-1, BMW 801 engines and at first no fewer than six MG 151/20s as fixed armament. Since the nose-mounted cannon tended to damage the radar when they were fired, they were later removed. In one of the first aerial battles between the Ju 88 G-1 and the RAF's Mosquito on 3 December 1943, both friend and foe suffered losses: three Ju 88 Gs and two Mosquitoes went down. The Ju 88 G-1 with the GM-1 injection system was produced in limited numbers as special version R-1.

Its successor, the Ju 88 G-2, included components of the Ju 88 G-1, Ju 188 A-2/G-2 and the Ju 388. Up to the wings and the Jumo 213 engines, the aircraft was identical to the Ju 88 G-1. The Ju 88 G-3 provided an interim solution before the availability of the Jumo 213 E. This night fighter had the Ju 88 A-4 wing and was powered by two DB 603 E engines. Only one prototype, the Ju 88 V 105 (Works No 710523) was built. The Ju 88 G-4 was a heavy fighter with Jumo 213 A engines but did not go into production. The Ju 88 G-5 was cancelled on 2 March 1944 since production of the Ju 88 G-2 was expected in the near future.

Apart from the Ju 88 G-1, the G-6 series was the only one to go into large-scale production. The mass-produced aircraft had four forward-firing MG 151s and two 'Schräge Musik' mountings ('slanting or Jazz music': code-name for dorsally mounted guns intended

to fire upwards into bomber formations). Apart from the powerplant it was virtually identical to the Ju 88 G-1. Most of the series were fitted with FuG 220 radar. At the end of 1944 several Ju 88 G-6 prototypes were tried out with the Morgenstern aerial array and 'Berlin Gerät'.

The G-7 was an extension of the G-6 series and had Ju 188 wings and Jumo 213 E engines with extra injection (MW 50) and four-bladed propellers.

In addition to the Ju 88 G-7 high-performance night fighter, a special 'Mosquito-destroyer' was produced in limited numbers. The first two prototypes were delivered on 6 November 1944 but before they could fly they were destroyed in a night bombing raid on Dessau on 7/8 March 1945. Two further examples were still being worked on in April 1945. The last of the Ju 88 G series was assembled at Merseburg in early 1945 and designated Ju 88 G-10. Intended as long-range night fighters, these aircraft were used mainly in connection with the 'Mistel' composite aircraft programme at the end of the war.

Above: Only the first few aircraft of the Ju 88 G-1 series were fitted with six MG 151/20s as fixed armament. Four guns were more usual in later models.

Right: This Ju 88 G-6, attached to 7./NJG 100, had only one MG 151/20 as fixed armament. The MG 131 fitted in the dorsal position was equipped with a flare-shield.

Left: A Ju 88 G-1 of NJG 3 equipped with FuG 220 radar.

Right: A Ju 88 G-1 (Works No 713521) at the end of the war.

Messerschmitt Bf 110 C/F/G

At the beginning of the war the heavy fighter (Zerstörer) was a completely new concept in armed aircraft, with major roles as escort for bombers and support for ground troops. However, due to its tactical inferiority to single-engined enemy fighters, as the war progressed the Bf 110 was used increasingly as a night fighter. Deliveries of the Bf 110 C-1 with DB 601 A-1 engines began in 1940. The C-2 series had MG FF cannon replacing the two nose-mounted MG 151/20 guns. The first victories over enemy four-engined bombers took place on the night of 10 April 1941 (Short Stirling) and 24 June of the same year (Handley Page Halifax). Their power advantage over their opponents was in fact very small. In February 1941, Bf 110 production reached its peak but from January 1942 fell to zero, since by then the night fighter version of the Me 210 was coming on line. In the summer of 1942 losses were still barely

being replaced. Improved types such as the Bf 110 F-2/F-3 with DB 601 F engines and three-man crews, with upward-firing weapons and enlarged rudders, finally reached the Geschwadern.

From 1943 the Bf 110 was seen as only a temporary solution, while waiting for the more powerful Heinkel He 219. Meanwhile, new Bf 110 night fighters had reached the production stage, such as the G-2 equipped with two MG 151s and four nose-mounted MG 17s. As additional armament either two MG 151s or BK 3.7 37mm cannon could be fitted beneath the fuselage. Deliveries of the considerably improved Bf 110 G with DB 605 B-1 engines began in 1942. Parallel to this came the F-series not much more than a year later. The Bf 110 G-1 was produced in only small numbers and was followed by the G-2 series as a heavy fighter and tank destroyer. Fixed armament consisted of four MG 17s and two MG

Right: The Bf 110 V4 of 14./NJG 5 was, up to April 1944, equipped with FuG 212 radar.

Below: These Bf 110 G-4/R1s (coded 'D5+LT') fitted with Lichtenstein BC airborne radar flew with NJG 3.

151/20s, with additional armament type M 1 with two MG 151/20s in fuselage turrets, or type M 2 with WGr 21 rocket-launchers under the wings. This version could be used as a fighter-bomber.

At the same time came the gradual replacement of the inadequate MG 17s by heavier MK 108 cannon. A model with the new armament configuration was produced by the Gothaer Waggonfabrik. The first prototypes were credited with 32 victories while serving with IV./Nachtjagdgeschwader 1 between 2 April and 27 May 1944. Within the Bf 110 G-3 series there was also a reconnaissance aircraft and fighter-bomber with photographic equipment and provision for a bomb rack.

The Bf 110 G-4 night fighter was powered by two DB 603 engines. For navigation it was equipped with the FuG 16 ZE with APZA-6 direction finder, and as recognition radar the FuG 25 A and the FuG 220 Lichtenstein equipment. An increase in rudder size was necessary to compensate for the Lichtenstein's aerial array. Armament and fuel system were largely similar to those of the G-2 series, with the MG 151/20s often favoured as the upward-firing armament. No suitable place could then be found for the MG 81 Z rear defence machine-guns.

The limits of performance were reached with the Bf 110 G-4/U7 night fighter, which had SN 2 radar, a GM 1 nitrous oxide injection system and its fuselage extended by 0.6m. Test

Right: Feldwebel Kustusch of 6./NJG 2 in front of his 'R4+BP'.

flights were made by NJG 1. In many cases the upward-firing MG 151s were replaced by MG FF cannon, as these were readily available. In 1943 practical tests took place with several 30mm weapons, the MK 101 and nose armament consisting of two MK 108s and one MK 103. One prototype flew between August and December 1943.

Most Bf 110 C aircraft served with NJG 1 and 3, with F and G models going to NJG 2, 3, 5 and 6. The Bf 110 G also served with Air Observation Squadrons 1 to 7 as well as night fighter squadrons in Norway and Finland.

Left: The Bf 110 G-4/R4 had four nose-mounted MG 151/20 cannon in place of two MK 108s. This aircraft, seen in the summer of 1944, was attached to 5./NJG 5.

Right: A Bf 110 G-4 attached to IV./NJG

Right: Several Bf 110 G-4s of NJG 2 were given an additional armoured windscreen to provide more protection for the pilot.

Right: Two Bf 110 G-4/R3s of 7./NJG 3, equipped with FuG 220 radar.

Left: Cockpit interior of a Bf 110 G-4 with a magazine (MG FF) for the upward-firing cannon.

Right: This Bf 110 G-4 ('B4+KA') was attached to a night fighter squadron in Norway.

Left: Night fighter of IV./NJG 2 with clearly visible flare-shields on the sides of the engines.

Right: Service aircraft of II./ZG 1 (later III./ZG 76) jacked up for gun tests at the butts.

Left: Well camouflaged aircraft parks became a necessity during the Allied air attacks from 1944. The aircraft in this case is a Bf 110 G-4 of NJG 1.

Right: A Bf 110 F-2 of ZG 26 with an MG 81Z machine-gun for rear defence.

Above left: Training flight over southern Germany in summer 1942.

Left: Service aircraft of ZG 1 ('2J+AR') for use as a fighter-bomber with fuselage-mounted ETC.

Above: The aircraft park of Zerstörergeschwader ZG 1.

Above right: Servicing the nose armament which consisted of two MG FFs and four MG 17s, at Augsburg.

Right: A jacked-up Bf 110 C-3 of ZG 26.

Below right: Aircrew of ZG 26.

Above: A Bf 110 G-2/R2 of I./ZG 76 armed with WGr 21 rocket-launchers during the defence of the Reich, in which the squadron incurred heavy losses.

Left: This Bf 110 G-2 of 7./ZG 26 is also equipped with a WGr 21 rocket-launcher, in this case with only two tubes.

Left: Factory testing of the Bf 110's ZFR 3 sight.

Right: Test installation of an MG 131 for rear defence.

Right: A Bf 110 G-2/R4 with two MG 151/20s in place of the previous nose armament, as well as a 37mm cannon mounted beneath the fuselage, seen at Munich-Riem in June 1944).

Below: A Bf 110 G-2 of the heavy-fighter reserve group.

Heinkel He 219

As early as August 1940 the Heinkel design office was planning several versions of a new twin-engined aircraft including a high-speed bomber (Project P 1056) and a reconnaissance aircraft (P 1055), to which was soon added, on the order of the Air Ministry, a multi-seat high-altitude reconnaissance aircraft. Later the project was continued as 'Reconnaissance Plane' and 'Day Bomber'. In November 1940 a heavy-fighter variant was introduced. This aircraft was intended to have a defensive armament consisting of up to eight movable and two fixed guns. By the beginning of 1941 there was also a heavily armed escort fighter version, and in the summer of 1941 a night fighter version was developed.

In August 1941 the design was given the designation He 219. A few months later, in November, the Chancellor himself was able to inspect the first model via the Air Ministry. On 7 April 1942 the final model inspection took place. The components were produced up to September and final assembly of the first prototype began. Before this, the decision had already been taken to concentrate the whole of

Below: The He 219 A-053 was similarly equipped to the A-5/R1, with the addition of FuG 212 and FuG 220 radar.

the He 219 development programme at Vienna-Schwechat.

After initial taxiing trials, test pilot Peter took the He 219 V 1 model ('VG+LW') on its first flight on 6 November 1942, and on 10 January 1943 the V 2 ('GG+WG') flew. Service units began to receive the He 219 in March 1943, but the intended remote-controlled defensive armament was removed and the airframe extended. Because of the increased length and the enlarged twin rudders, stability about the main axis was poor, there was vibration in both fuselage and rudder, and

severe changes in trim occurred when the landing flaps were extended. Prototypes V 7 to V 9 went for service testing to Venlo in Holland and the zero-series aircraft began to appear from July 1943. The He 219 V 9 began to see tough service from June 1943.

However, a fully equipped He 219 Gruppe remained an illusion at first, as did the 2,000 He 219s which had been ordered, or the rapid transfer from the zero-series to the He 219 A-2. Even Professor Heinkel's vehement demands for more qualified workers for the series production were not enough; in August 1943

Right: Final assembly of an He 219 A-0.

monthly output was still only ten night fighters.

Meanwhile, however, the first He 219 A-5 became available and its armament and performance were convincing. At NJG 1 in Venlo (Commander Hauptmann Meurer) the He 219 was given an extremely good report. Because of cutbacks, the aircraft could not be armed with the intended MK 103 and MK 108, so the readily available MG 151 was used instead. In July 1944 the first He 219 A-7 was given service trials. The B and C series remained on the drawing-board except for test aircraft. The He 219 D and E did not reach the project stage.

Versions worth mentioning include the He 219 V 18 with four-bladed propellers and Jumo 222 A/B engines, and the He 219 V 28 ('VO+BC') and V 31 ('DV+DB') with braking parachute for landing. An ejection seat was tested in He 219 V 6, which was later given Works No 190113 ('DV+DI'). On 19 November 1942 General Kammhuber allowed himself to be shot to a height of 4m at 6g acceleration on a ground rig in order to gain an impression of the Heinkel ejection seat.

The trial objectives of test aircraft were often changed. So, for example, an A-0/R-6 was first used as the test model designated He 219 V 16, followed by an A-5 which had an SN-2 radar system. Eventually these aircraft and the V 19 were fitted with upward-firing weapons and given to NJG 1. The V 28 ('RL+AH') was the forerunner of the He 219 A-5/R-3, and the aircraft arrived at Venlo in June 1944. For the prototype trials it was fitted with DB 603 G engines, and in July 1944 the V 25 flew as a three-seat A-5/R-4.

During the same month Director Francke gave the following results of power trials: maximum speed of the He 219 with DB 603 A engines, SN-2 aerial and flare-suppression equipment (Fla-V-Anlage), was around 585km/h. Heinkel hoped for a further improvement in performance with the installation of more powerful engines. However, the Jumo 222 was not available in series production, and there were numerous problems with both the DB 603 L and the Jumo 213 with MW 50 injection.

A maximum speed of 620km/h at 7,500m had been attained using Jumo 222 A/B engines. With Jumo 222 E/Fs and improved Lichtenstein aerials, maximum speed was to be increased by 46km/h at 11,500m fully pressurized altitude. It was also hoped to obtain an additional 5 per cent power increase by the use of methanol-water injection, although only at greater altitudes. In the event, the A-2 with Jumo 213 Es derived from the standard engine achieved only 635km/h, and as little as 605km/h without methanol injection. The use of this engine also involved considerable structural alterations to the mountings, cowling, exhaust and lubrication system, as well as to the fuel tank connections. Finally, six machines were equipped with Jumo 213 Es with methanol injection by the end of 1944, although the Junkers engine factory was having problems with the supercharger. Because of overloading of the supercharger drive gear, supply to service units was a long way off even at the beginning of 1945. Without methanol injection the power was not significantly higher than with DB 603 engines, so it was never possible for the He 219 to reach performance levels comparable with those of the Mosquito.

During the period 1943 to March 1945, Heinkel produced 268 aircraft of the He 219 series as so-called 'newbuildings'. A further six machines were assembled from surplus parts. Some 27 night fighters which had suffered considerable damage were refitted and returned to active service. The Luftwaffe received only 195 He 219s, most of which went to NJG 1; the remaining machines were used mainly for test purposes or were lost in enemy air attacks. In combat, 46 He 219s were destroyed and a further seventeen were badly damaged.

The A-0 version, with over 100 aircraft, was the most numerous of the He 219 series. As a night fighter with greater range, the He 219 A-2 came into use in quite large numbers. Further, according to a plan of 22 December 1944, 210 of the A-7 series were to be built between December 1944 and July 1945. The first five of these aircraft were to have DB 603 Aa engines and the rest the more powerful DB 603 E. In fact, only a few He 219 A-7s were ever produced.

Despite the relatively small numbers available, the He 219 night fighter was remarkably effective. Altogether 111 enemy aircraft were shot down by He 219s between 12 June 1943 and 25 June 1944. The first major use of the He 219 was by NJG 1 at Venlo, which had already tested the V 7 and V 9 models in May 1943 (by XII. Fliegerkorps). Up to 6 November 1944, I./NJG 1 itself claimed more than 130 kills, of which however only eleven were Mosquitoes.

Above: An He 219 ready for delivery from the Heinkel factory at Oranienburg.

Summary of the He 219

Model	Equipment	Engines	Armament	Radar
A-0/R1	Fuselage extension for V model, normal wing, two-man cockpit	DB603A	2 MK 108s in ventral tray, 2 MG 151s in wing roots,conversion packs M1-M3	FuG 212 C1
A-0/R2	As A-0/R1, stronger undercarriage	DB603A	4 MK 103s in ventral tray	Fug 212 C1
A-0/R3	Model for A-2 series, improved A-0	DB603A	4 MK 103s in ventral tray, 2 MG 151s in wing roots	FuG 212 C2
A-0/R6	Model for A-5 series	DB 603A	4 MK 108s in ventral tray, 2 MG 151s in wing roots, 2 upward-firing MK 108s, Conversion packs M1-M3	FuG 212 and FuG 220
A-1	Planned main series for A-0, recessed two-man cockpit	DB 603A/B		

Model	Equipment	Engines	Armament	Radar
A-2/R1	Improved A-0, single-core wiring, two-man cockpit, extra range	DB 603A/B	2 MK 103s in ventral tray, 2 MG 151s in wing roots, 2 Upward-firing MK 108s	FuG 220
A-2/R2	As A-2/R1, test on flare-suppressor	DB 603A/B	As A-2/R1	FuG 220
A-3	Further development of A-2 with 900-litre drop-tank, minimum standard equipment, two-man cockpit, planned bomber	DB 603E/F DB 603 G	2 MK 108s in wing roots. Planned for upward-firing armament	
A-4	Further development of A-2 as Mosquito-killer and reconnaissance aircraft less armour and armament, GM-1 + turbocharger, two-man cockpit	DB 603A/B Jumo 222	2 MK 108s in wing roots, 2 MK 103s in ventral tray	
A-5/R1	Further development of A-3, earlier designation A-0/R6	DB 603A	2 MG 151s in wing roots, 2 MK 108s in ventral tray, 2 upward-firing Mk 108s	FuG 212 and FuG 220
A-5/R2	Prototype for A-7/R4	DB 603A	2 MG 151s in wing roots, 2 MG 151s in ventral tray 2 upward-firing MK 108s	FuG 220

Left: The first Heinkel He 219 (Works No 219001, 'VG+LW') was used mainly for flight testing.

Model	Equipment	Engines	Armament	Radar
A-5/R3	Series design based on He 219 V 28	DB 603E	2 MG 151s in wing roots, 2 MG 103s in ventral tray, 2 upward-firing MK 108s	FuG 220
A-5/R4	Development of A-3 with three-man cockpit, extra range, defensive armament based on He 219 V 34	DB 603E	2 MG 151s in wing roots, 2 MG 151s in ventral tray, 2 upward-firing MK 108s, Defensive armament in turret possible	FuG 220
A-6	Unarmoured version of He 219 A-2	DB 603E	2 MG 151s in wing roots, 2 MG 151s in ventral tray	FuG 220
A-7/R1	Improved series design based on He 219 V 25	DB 603G	2 MK 108s in wing roots, 2 MG 151s and 2 MK 103s in ventral tray	FuG 220
A-7/R2	Series version with upward-firing armament; proto-type: He 219 V 26	DB 603G	Armament as A-7/R1 with 2 upward-firing MK 108s	FuG 220
A-7/R3	Pre-series for planned B-1 series; prototype: He 219 V 27	DB 603G	2 MG 151s in wing roots, 2 MG 151s in ventral tray, 2 MK 108s as upward-firing armament in fuselage	FuG 220
A-7/R4	Design with reduced armament	DB 603G	2 MG 151s in wing roots, 2 MG 151s in ventral tray	FuG 220
A-7/R5	Mosquito-destroyer with methanol injection system	Jumo 213E	2 MG 151s in wing roots, 2 MG 151s in ventral tray	
A-7/R6	Test-bed for Jumo 222A; prototype: He 219 V 18	Jumo 222A	2 MG 151s in wing roots, 4 MK 108s in ventral tray	

Left: Close-up of the nose-wheel of an He 219 A-0.

Above: Crash of the He 219 V2 ('GG+WG'), which flew for the first time on 10 January 1943.

Below: Two MG 151/20 cannon in the wing roots of an He 219 A-0.

Focke-Wulf Ta 154

After the heavy nightly air raids by the RAF in the early summer of 1942, the German Air Ministry ordered the building of a more powerful night fighter. Heinkel, Focke-Wulf and Junkers were asked to produce a design for a two-seat all-weather night fighter with an endurance of two to three hours and armament consisting of four forward-firing cannon. The aircraft was to be built as a small series with the simplest possible construction, and was to use minimal amounts of steel and aluminium. By using existing mass-produced engines, the first flight was required to be made within twelve months.

In September 1942 Kurt Tank, Chief Designer of Focke-Wulf, produced a design for a two-seat night fighter made entirely from wood and with a nose wheel undercarriage. Two months later he received an order 'With Maximum Urgency' from the Technical Division. Direct competitors to the Ta 154 were the He 219 and Ju 388 J. On 1 July 1943 the Ta 154 V 1 made its first flight at Hannover-Langenhagen with Hans Sander as test pilot. Without equipment or armament the aircraft reached a speed of 635km/h at an altitude of 6,000m using Jumo 211 engines - the Jumo 213 was still not available. Later the machine was armed first with two MG 151/20s and two MK 108s. To obtain reliable values for the stiffness of the forward fuselage and cockpit area, 'barge tests' (underwater drag-testing) were carried out in Lake Alatsee near Füssen by the Luftfahrt-Forschungsanstalt Graf

Right: Wind-tunnel model of the Focke-Wulf Ta 154 heavy fighter/night fighter.

Below: Side-view of the Ta 154 V-1. Only twelve prototypes of the Ta 154, together with a few series aircraft and five spare airframes, were produced.

Zeppelin (FGZ) Research Establishment.

The second prototype was fitted with FuG 212 'Lichtenstein C-1' radar, and was also used for flight testing to obtain additional static vibration data. The first pre-production aircraft, the Ta 154 V 3 (Ta 154 A-03/U1), was powered by Jumo 213 A engines. Because of the weight of armament and equipment, and the full radar installation with four nose-mounted aerials, the top speed dropped by 75km/h despite the higher engine power. Nevertheless, an order was placed for over 250 Ta 154 A-1 aircraft.

Towards the end of 1943 the Ta 154 V 4 to V 7 prototypes were built by Focke-Wulf at Langenhagen, and in early 1944 these aircraft were given certificates of airworthiness. The first eight pre-series aircraft were built by the Gothaer Waggonfabrik in early 1944 at the Salzbergwerk Wremen.

The first production Ta 154 A-1 flew on 13 June 1944. The A-1 series was intended to be built at Wremen, while production of wings and undercarriages began at the Posen factory in Poland, and the fuselage with its pressurized

cabin was simultaneously produced at Cottbus. At around this time bombing raids destroyed the firm of Goldman, which had produced the 'Tego Film' aircraft adhesive used for the TA 154's wooden components. Focke-Wulf therefore turned to Dynamit AG at Leverkusen for supplies of another adhesive, but this was still in the development stage and was only half as powerful. Professor Tank therefore decided to stop production. Since the Ta 154 programme would suffer considerable delays until an improved adhesive was available, the Air Ministry withdrew the order for series production and redeployed the underground production facility at Salzbergwerk Wremen. Only seven examples of the Ta 154 A-1 were built.

With Jumo 213 A engines the Ta 154 was still capable of 630km/h at an altitude of 8,500m; the Mosquito with its Rolls-Royce Merlin 21s could achieve 620km/h at 6,300m. The Ta 154 could attack Mosquitoes only at safe altitudes — not much of an advantage! Only with the use of the Jumo 213 E and GM-1 injection could this advantage be increased.

Left: Full-scale mock-up of the Ta 154, showing one of the six guns which formed its offensive armament, as well as the FuG 212 radar.

Left: Works Nos 320008 to 320010 were equipped as all-weather fighters (A-2/U4). Four aircraft were converted to night fighters designated Ta 154 A-4 shortly before the end of the war.

Left: Professor Kurt Tank stepping out of the first prototype Ta 154 at Hannover-Langenhagen on 7 July 1943.

Jet Aircraft

Right: Pilots of JG 1 assembled around their He 162 A-1/A-2s waiting for the British occupying forces on 6 May 1945.

Below: The He 280 V-2 ('GJ+CA') was destroyed on 26 June 1943 after an engine failure.

Heinkel He 280

In response to the Air Ministry Directive of 4 January 1939, Heinkel drew up the first design for a gas turbine-powered pursuit fighter with three MG 151/20 cannon as fixed armament. In the summer of 1939 two different models were produced of a fighter which was first designated He 180. On 26 September Air Ministry representatives inspected the mock-ups at the Rechlin Test Establishment, and from then on the aircraft was referred to as the He 280. As with other aircraft manufacturers, serious problems were encountered with the jet engines in terms of operational safety. It would be years before either the BMW P 3302 or the HeS 8A would be completely trouble-free. Meanwhile there were tests on the armament and ejection seat.

On 28 August 1940 the He 280 V1 was rolled out at Rostock-Marienehe and a month later it made an unpowered towed test flight,

being towed into the air by a Heinkel He 111. By the end of 1940 the second prototype was in final assembly, and the He 280 V3 to V5 were partially complete. Heinkel was also trying to obtain a firm order from the Air Ministry for further test models up to V10. As there seemed to be no immediate prospect of either a fully functional BMW P 3302 or HeS 8A gas turbine, the possibility of using a pulse-jet was investigated. The first flight of the He 280 V2 with two HeS 8A engines took place on 30 March 1941. In June 1942 an Argus As 014 pulse-jet for the He 280 V1 was delivered to Rostock. By the end of October, the first prototype was equipped with four of these pulse-jets and at that point tests with the Heinkel jet engine were discontinued.

In July 1942 the He 280 V3 made its first flight using HeS 8A engines, although these were later replaced by two Jumo 004s. By the

Right: The He 280 V-3 ('GJ+CB') flew for the first time on 5 July 1942 and was powered by two HeS 8A jet engines.

Below right: The He 280 V-3 was put into store after the end of development at Vienna and remained there until May 1945.

Below: The He 280 V-1 first prototype made its first flight on 22 September 1940. The aircraft crashed, after 64 towed flights, on 13 January 1943.

winter of 1942 plans for 24 test models of the He 280 with Jumo and BMW jet engines had been drawn up. The He 280 V10 to V24 were designated as production series He 280 B-1s, which were to be provided with heavier nose armament (six guns). In addition, the possibility of adding a jettisonable rack beneath the fuselage centre-section was investigated. Because of high fuel consumption, the airframe had to be enlarged. Also the twin rudders had to be replaced by a single central rudder for production reasons. However, the He 280 fell behind the Me 262 on the basis of power calculations, and the Messerschmitt fighter was already further into its test programme. For these reasons, no further models of the He 280 were built after the V9 and in March 1943 the Air Ministry cancelled the production order. The remaining He 280s served mainly to test new rudder forms and most of the aircraft were later stored.

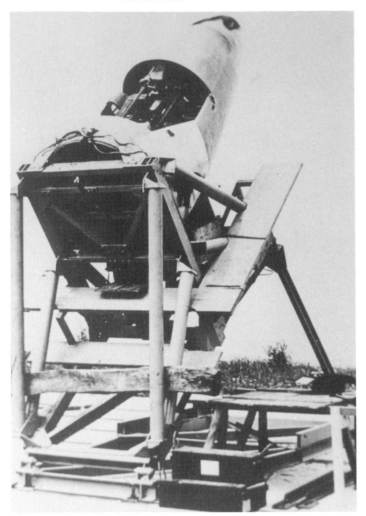

Above left and right: The test rig for the weapons platform of the He 280 B-1 during a static test at the factory.

Left: Three MG 151 cannon were intended as the armament for the planned He 280 B-1 series.

Summary of Heinkel He 280 Prototypes

Model	Code	First Flight	Engine	Remarks
V 1	'OL+AS'	22.09.1940	Unpowered	Crashed 13.01.1943 after 64 towed flights
		01.04.1941	HeS 8A	Airworthiness tests only
		13.01.1943	As 014	
V 2	'GJ+CA'	30.03.1941	HeS 8A	
		16.03.1943	Jumo 004	80 per cent damage following engine failure on 26.06.1943
V 3	'GJ+CB'	05.07.1942	HeS 8A	Components available in April 1945 at Schwechat
V 4	—	13.08.1943	BMW 003	Airworthiness only
		31.09.1944	Jumo 004	Airworthiness only, airframe at Hörsching in October 1944
V 5	—	26.07.1943	He S8A	Airworthiness only
		15.09.1943	BMW 003	Airworthiness only. Airframe stored in parts
V 6	—	26.07.1943	BMW 003	Airworthiness. Airframe stored in parts
V 7	'NU+EB' 'D-IXEM'	19.04.1943	Unpowered	115 towed flights to beginning of 1945
V 8	'NU+EC'	19.07.1943	Jumo 004	
		15.08.1943	He TL	Airworthiness only. In possession of DFS March 1945
V 9	—	31.08.1943	BMW 003	Airworthiness only. Airframe stored in parts
V 10	—	April 1943	Jumo 004	Planned airworthiness; first prototype He 280 B-1
V 11	—	May 1943	HMW 003A	Planned airworthiness; second prototype He 280 B-1s
V 12	—	June 1943	He TL	Planned airworthiness; third prototype He 280 B-1s

Messerschmitt Me 262

The design for the Messerschmitt Me 262 arose from the Me P 65/P 1065 project of 15 December 1938 for a 'High-Speed Fighter Aircraft for Operation Against Aerial Targets'. Flight tests began in April 1941 with a single Jumo 210 G piston engine installed in the nose. This was replaced by two BMW P 3302 turbojets as soon as their performance was deemed acceptable. On 25 March 1942 the V 1 took off using its jet engines, which however had a very short endurance so that the

aircraft, which still retained its piston engine, had to land under propeller power. In the summer of 1942 the construction of five prototypes was authorized, for production in 1943. The V-prototypes had Jumo 004 engines, after it had been established that the power of the BMW gas turbine did not meet requirements.

During a meeting in August 1942, an increase in the number of V-prototypes to ten was requested by KdE. The power and

Right: The first production Me 262 (S-1, Works No 130006, 'VI+AF'), which made its maiden flight on 19 April 1944 and was used mainly for weapons testing.

Below: This Me 262 A-1a (Works No 500079) was discovered by Allied troops at Giebelstadt on 4 April 1945. The machine had presumably belonged to KG(J) 54 and came originally from KG 51.

reliability of the jet engines were still not acceptable, so that flight tests with a few aircraft were possible at Messerschmitt only after some delays. Production conditions for these aircraft were established in March 1943, with equipment details following in Messerschmitt Factory Protocol No 11 of 28 May 1943. The construction of 100 Me 262 test models and zero-series aircraft was then approved by a KdE order of 10 April 1943 so as to complete testing on a broader basis. Out of this barely satisfactory situation arose the production order, which, on the cancellation of the Me 209, had been made on 25 May 1943 by Generalfeldmarschall Milch after consultations with Reichsmarschall Göring.

Up to May 1943, four Me 262s had been produced, all fitted with tail wheels. The test models not yet available (V 5 to V 10) were to be built through to March 1944, so the Me 262 V 5 became the first test model, in the summer of 1943, to be fitted with a nose wheel, though it was non-retractable. On 1 October 1942 the Me 262 V 2 made its first flight powered by Jumo 004 engines. It was followed into the air by Me 262 V 3 on 17 July, also with Jumo 004s. Testing of the V 4 began in April 1943.

Despite strenuous efforts, little useful data had been obtained up to December 1943 because so few aircraft were available. The KdE and GdJ therefore organized the establishment of Erprobungskommando Me 262 (Test Command) at Lechfeld airfield under the command of Hauptmann Thierfelder. The first aircraft supplied to the Erprobungskommando was the Me 262 V 5 with fixed undercarriage. It was used mainly

for training and apart from nose wheel tests yielded hardly any results. Performance and power trials began with the sixth and seventh prototypes which had been supplied meanwhile. With a large degree of participation by the firm Junkers at their Rechlin test establishment, engine tests of the Jumo 004 began. Considerable delays were experienced in the programme due to engine failures. At the same time, armament tests began, carried out selectively by Kommando Me 262 with the participation of the Rechlin and Tarnewitz test establish-ments.

The aircraft in the production programme of 16 June 1943 were regarded as a pre-production series. However, this did not come to fruition due to air raids on Messerschmitt's Augsburg and Regensburg factories. The series was further delayed by technical difficulties from the middle of January to the end of March 1944. To keep risks to the minimum, all technical departments were to be co-ordinated by the Model Supervisor. The intention was to bring together all necessary documents and test results as early as possible, in order to avoid further delays in the progress of the series. An important factor in this preliminary work was the establishment of a Stress Test Commission by Generalfeldmarschall Milch. This Commission consist-ed of delegates from the DVL, E-Stelle, and qualified engineers from the aircraft industry. Their work was especially important since the vibration and stress tests at Augsburg had been interrupted by enemy action. Production, which had started in March 1944, was again interrupted on 24 April by bombing raids on Leipheim. The first five

Final assembly of the zero-series of the Me 262 at Leipheim.

Left: Ground crew of the Me 262 at Lechfeld near Landsberg. In the background is a six-engined Me 323.

Right: All Me 262 A-1as were modified as auxiliary 'Blitz Bombers'.

production aircraft were produced by the E-Kommando in collaboration with Messerschmitt.

At Whitsun, during a meeting with the Reichsmarschall at Obersalzberg — and on a decision by the Führer himself — it was decided that the Me 262, which had been developed as a fighter and fighter-bomber, should become a 'Blitzbomber'. This command to produce a 'Maximum-Speed Bomber' produced, during the threatened invasion of France, an accelerated test programme which was inevitably limited to necessities and front-line applications.

The emergency tests carried out at the Rechlin Research Establishment covered the technical usefulness for the role of 'Maximum-Speed Bomber'. Most tests were carried out at Rechlin-Lärz. The EKL took over servicing of the aircraft and the task of organizing flying operations. The tests included power trials (E 2), range tests with two 250kg and one 500kg bombs (E 2), take-off tests with bombs and two RI 502s (E 2), engine tests with six aircraft at EKL Lärz and with two aircraft at E 3 (E 3), radar and target spotting tests (E 4), tests on hydraulic and electrical equipment as well as on course steering (component testing for fighter control and bombing) (E 5), bomb and loading trials for two 250kg (BT 200c) or one 500kg and BT 400, tests of the BZA bombsight installation and bombing pattern (E 7), as well as the use of various towing machinery and towing harnesses for nose-wheel aircraft and supercharged-engine transport vehicles (E 8). The BZA sight proved unsatisfactory so the TSA 2 was to be installed and tested. The course steering equipment was necessary, and additional tanks were to be installed to increase range.

The tests at Rechlin began on 10 June 1944 when the first aircraft became available. Delivery of twelve further Me 262s continued until July 1944. Undercarriage problems delayed the test programme by a further four weeks. However, by 20 September 1944, 350 flying hours and over 800 take-offs had been recorded at Rechlin. The service capability of the aircraft as a fighter was reported by telegram to the KdE on 12 September 1944. At the same time results of fighter tests, including nine 'kills', were also advised.

The evaluation of flying characteristics and performance after the tests gave satisfactory roll rate, and also good stability about the main axis. The high control forces above 600km/h, however, made it necessary to install a trim control for fighter application. This was introduced on the 146th machine. In general, the aircraft was easy to fly and exhibited no tendency to yaw to either side. Take-offs and landings as a fighter could be carried out by an average pilot. The only extra pilot training needed was with respect to the jet engine.

All-round pilot visibility was excellent; the windscreen had already proved itself. Positive instrument and blind-flying properties were established over many night and bad-weather trials. Improvements were also made in the landing gear, and as a result landing weight could be increased from 5,300 to

5,700kg. Take-off weight in the 'Blitzbomber' role was normally around 7,100kg. For use as a 'Blitzbomber', two of the four cannon were removed and the gun apertures sealed.

Functional tests of bombing capability were carried out by arrangement between the E-Stelle and Messerschmitt for amendments to the Messerschmitt ('Viking Ship') rack. In the series construction, the ETC 504 rack was used as it was capable of carrying the required drop load. On the 'Viking Ship', the SC 250, SD 250, AB 250-2, SC 500, SD 500 and AB 500-1 could be carried, but not the AB 500-3, BT 200 or ER 4 Schloss 50. On the ETC 504 or 503, the SC 250, SD 250, AB 250-2, SD 500, SC 500, AB 500-1, AB 500-3 and BT 200 could be carried. Only the BT 400 could not be carried as it protruded over the undercarriage fairings. Bombs of 50kg could only be carried with the AB 500-3.

Below: This Me 262 was attached to Erprobungskommando (Jagd) [Fighter Test Command], which was transferred to the Nowotny Kommando, which later became III.(Erg)/JG 2.

Bottom: An Me 262 A-1a of JV 44 (Galland) in service at Munich.

Summary of Me 262

Me 262 A-1a Jet fighter with two Jumo 004B engines

Me 262 A-1b Jet fighter with two BMW 003B engines

Me 262 A-1a/R-1 Equipped with R4M rockets as armament

Me 262 A-1/Bo Auxiliary 'Blitzbomber'

Me 262 A-1a/U1 Mixed armament with two MK 103, MK 108 and MG 151 (planned series construction)

Me 262 A-1a/U2 All-weather fighter with FuG 125

Me 262 A-1a/U3 Unarmed reconnaissance version (modification of Me 262 A-1a)

Me 262 A-1a/U4 Heavy jet fighter with 50mm MK 214

Me 262 A-1a/U5 Heavy jet fighter with six nose-mounted MK 108s

Below: JV 44 had 55 confirmed kills to its credit.

Bottom: One of some 180 Me 262 A-1as ('B3+GR') delivered in March 1945 to Kampfgeschwader (Jagd) 54 at Neuburg/Donau.

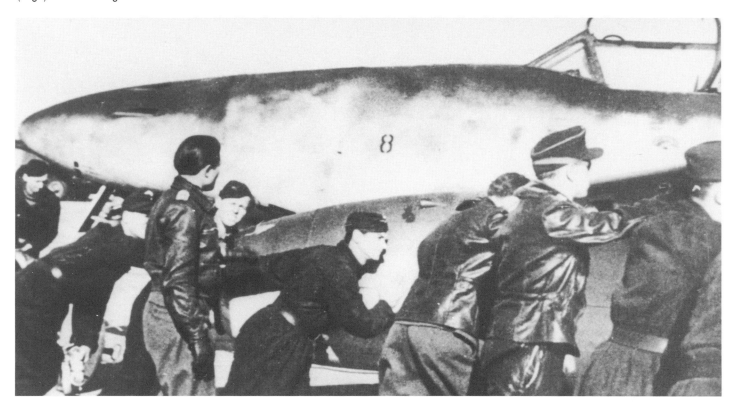

Me 262 A-2a 'Blitzbomber' with reduced armament (two MK 108s)

Me 262 A-2a/R 'Blitzbomber' with reinforced armour

Me 262 A-2a/U1 'Blitzbomber' with TSA sight

Me 262 A-2a/U2 Two-seat high-speed bomber (Lotfe-Bomber)

Me 262 A-3a Armoured aircraft I and II

Me 262 A-4a Previous designation for Me 262 A-1a/U1 and A-1a/U3

Me 262 A-5a Armed reconnaissance aircraft

Me 262 B-1a Two-seat trainer

Me 262 B-1a/U1Z Two-seat auxiliary night fighter

Me 262 B-2a Two-seat night fighter with Jumo 004s

Me 262 C-1a Interceptor with two Jumo 004Bs and one rear-mounted HWK rocket engine (Heimatschutzer I)

Me 262 C-2b Interceptor with two BMW 003Rs (Heimatschutzer II)

Me 262 C-3a Interceptor with two Jumo 004Bs and one jettisonable HWK rocket engine mounted beneath the fuselage

De 262 D-1 Provisional designation for Me 262 C-2b

Me 262 E-1 Preliminary designation for Me 262 A-1a/U4

Me 262 S Zero-series model for Me 262 A-1a

Me 262 V Test model for Me 262

Me 262 W Provisional designation for Me 262 with pulse-jet engines

Conversion packs for the Me 262

R 1 Jettisonable rack under the fuselage for 500-litre fuel tank

R 2 JATO rocket (presumably RI-502) for overload take-off

R 3 Built-in, non-jettisonable rocket engine as additional thrust for the 'Heimatschutzer' (Project)

R 4 FuG 350 Zc 'Naxos' radar for night and bad-weather use (passive radar, corresponding to the British H2S radar), and FuG 218 'Neptun V' active target-seeking radar

R 5 Fixed armament MK 108

R 6 Fighter-bomber equipped with 503 A-1 bomb rack and TSA-D2 sight

R 7 Unguided R4M 'Orkan' air-to-air missile

R 8 Rheinmetall-Borsig R 100 BS unguided air-to-air rocket missile

R 9 Ruhrstahl 8-344 (X-4) wire-guided missile

Below: An Me 262 B-1a/U1 two-seat fighter of 7./KG (J) 54 during an engine test. In the cockpit is Oberfeldwebel Gentzsh.

Right: The 'Yellow 7' of III./JG 7 at Fürth in the early summer of 1945.

Below right: Fhr Hans-Guido Mütke of 9./JG 7 flew this aircraft (Works No 500071) to Switzerland on 24 April 1945.

Above left: Dismantling an Me 262 A-1a/R1. The R4M gratings under the wings are clearly visible.

Left: Changing an engine at Lechfeld. In the background is the Me 262 V-8.

Above: An aerial view of Lechfeld (taken by the US 8th Air Force) where the Me 262 was tested and where III.(Erg)/JG 2 was stationed from 1944.

Right: Lechfeld airfield in May 1945. On the left is the Me 262 V-12 (Works No 170074) without engines. This had formerly been designated the Me 262 C-2b powered by two BMW 003 R jet engines.

Left: One of the few Me 262 B-1a two-seaters. It was converted from an Me 262 A-1a by Blohm und Voss at Wesendorf.

Below left: Several destroyed Me 262 A-1a aircraft of KG(J) 54 were discovered at Neuburg/Donau in the summer of 1945.

Above: Production of Me 262s was transferred to the forest because of Allied air superiority

Below: American troops examine a damaged Me 262 A-1a of KG 51 at Frankfurt on 27 March 1945.

Heinkel He 162

Although in the Messerschmitt Me 262 the Luftwaffe had a powerful and highly developed jet aircraft, emphasis was still given to the development of other gas turbine-powered fighters. The Me 262 conformed to the quality criterion of the years 1940-1943, in that it was not then strictly necessary to keep production as simple as possible. At that time emphasis was on developing and producing everything to a 'schön und gut' (zero defects) standard.

After the change in priorities that placed fighters ahead of bombers, the increase in fighter production depended less upon the competitiveness of the airframe manufacturer and much more on the availability of constructional materials and fuel. Since these essentials were scarcer for the Germans than they were for the Allies, all possible economies and reductions had to be made.

In view of the aerial war situation, the training conditions for pilots, and the poor reliability of the jet engines then available, a long service life was not expected of jet aircraft. It was estimated that an Me 262 would be a total loss after five to ten missions. The Me 262, furthermore, required two jet engines and correspondingly more fuel, which in view of the rapidly worsening war situation was becoming increasingly scarce. The idea of building a single-engined jet fighter of about half the size, and therefore with similar performance, had much to commend it.

In the summer of 1944 Heinkel were already working on their Project P 1073, a high-speed jet fighter powered by one or two He 011 gas turbines. On 19 July that year, plans were also made for a jet fighter powered by a single BMW 003 engine. These developments were due mainly to the good

Left: The first prototype of the Messerschmitt P 1101. The aircraft is fitted with a model of the HeS 11 A-1 turbine.

Right: Model test of the Me P 1112/S-2, carried out in connection with the design of the Me P 1101/1110 and the 1111/1112. Development was in progress at the beginning of April 1945.

information supplied by Carl Frydag, Heinkel's General Director and close colleague of the Rüstungstab. On 8 September the Amt der Technischen Luftrüstung (Office of Air Technical Equipment, or TLR) produced the specification for a 'Volksjäger' (People's Fighter). Invitations to tender were given to the firms of Arado (E 580), Blohm und Voss (P 211), Dornier, Fieseler, Focke-Wulf ('Volksflitzer'), Heinkel (modified P 1073), Messerschmitt and Junkers (EF 123 and 124). The requirement was for a: gas turbine-powered fighter aircraft with the BMW 003 engine; employing the most economical construction method of wood and steel; maximum speed of 750km/h at sea-level; take-off distance to be not more than 500m; stable undercarriage for rough terrain; 30min endurance at 100 per cent thrust power at sea-level; instrumented for all-weather use, with

FuG 16 ZY or FuG 15 radar; armoured against 13mm shells for both pilot and ammunition; two MK 108 (100 rounds) or MG 151/20 (250 rounds) armament; fuel tank armour or provision for drop-tank; mass production with the simplest equipment; easy to fly; using as many components as possible of the Bf 109 or Fw 190 (this requirement was fulfilled by none of the firms!); suitable for transport by road; and with a total weight of not more than 2 tonnes.

Because they had already been working on the project, it took only three days for Heinkel to produce a design based on Project P 1073 for the Head of the TLR, and as early as 20 September 1944 the first prototype of the Volksjäger was produced. Nine days later the RMfRuK gave the order for production of the Volksjäger without waiting for test results. The first flight was to follow at the beginning of

Right: The only P 1101 to be completed was captured in damaged condition on 29 April 1945 when Oberammergau was occupied.

December 1944 and main production was to begin in the following March.

At the end of October, series production began and on 1 December the He 162 was ready for take-off. Taxiing tests began the next day, and on 6 December the He 162 V1 made its first flight at Schwechat-Heidfeld, near Vienna. This was made possible by the 1,360 Heinkel workers in Vienna working 90-hour weeks, later reduced to 70, as well as a system known as 'raschen Entscheidung' ('swift decision' — on-the-spot solutions to small problems).

The aircraft was a shoulder-wing design with a retractable nose-wheel undercarriage and was powered by a BMW 003 E engine with quick-release mountings so that it could be changed easily. The fuselage and rudder were of aluminium, the wings and tailplane of wood, with other components in steel. The Junkers-built He 162 A-1 was to have two 50-round MK 108s while the A2 series produced by Heinkel had two 120-round MG 151/20s. As the MK 108 had greater hitting power (one hit was considered to be enough to shoot down a Mustang, and three enough to shoot down a B-17), the A-1 was intended for action against bombers, with the A-2 reserved for anti-fighter attacks. Since by occupying Posen the Soviet

Army brought production of the MK 108 to a halt, the Volksjäger was produced only as the He 162 A-2.

The first prototype crashed on 10 December 1944, and further test flights with the He 162 V 2 led to strengthening of the wing skin. To reduce the aircraft's tendency to pitch-down, anhedral wing tips were installed, among other measures. To improve stability, Heinkel reduced the fuselage fuel tank and added weight to the nose, thus moving the centre of gravity forwards. The more elegant solution, an extension of the fuselage, was dismissed because of production difficulties. A further problem arose from the position of the engine, which was mounted above the fuselage. This meant that during turning manoeuvres the twin rudders could be affected by the jet exhaust, from which they could not then be moved, putting aircraft out of control.

On 14 January 1945 the first He 162 from Heinkel (EHAG-Nord) was produced at Rostock. At the end of the month DLH at Oranienburg undertook final assembly. Production at Rostock was held up because of lack of rudder components, and at Vienna barely twelve He 162s had been produced.

In February 1945 General der Jagdflieger Gollob planned to give clearance for the first

Above: The first prototype of the Heinkel He 162 V-1 (Works No 200001, 'VI+IA'), which first flew on 6 December 1944 piloted by Gotthold Peter.

Above: The first 'Volksjäger' (People's Fighter) produced by Junkers (JFM) on 23 March 1945.

Right: The first He 162 A-1 rolls off the production line at Heinkel's Oranienburg factory on 24 March 1945.

delivered to JG 1. Simultaneously models were made available to two squadrons (2. and 3./JG 1) for training purposes. These were located at Parchim and Heidfeld near Vienna. On 5 March 1945 the first test aircraft was delivered to the Test Establishment at Rechlin. By mid-March about 70 aircraft were under construction at the Junkers Bernburg factory, although they were held up by the lack of undercarriages. On 1 April 1945, I./JG 1 still had only four He 162s. A week later production of the He 162 was discontinued in favour of the Me 262 A-1.

On 11 April 1945, 2./JG 1 was transferred as Stabstaffel JG 1 from Lechfeld and Memmingen to serve as EKdo Lechfeld 162. For the first Gruppe, sixteen He 162s were now available. By the end of April the I.Einsatzgruppe/JG 1 was given clearance to use the Volksjäger, and several air battles followed between then and 5 May 1945. The only confirmed 'kill' was credited to Lt. R. Schmitt who on 4 May shot down a Typhoon. The British pilot was taken prisoner, and became a guest in the Staff Officers' Mess. No one dealt with him badly when he showed his pleasure at the news that British tanks were already at Leck. On 6 May the base was occupied by British troops. A few days previously, on 1 May, the squadron had 40 He 162s on charge, of which 30 were serviceable.

combat flight of the aircraft in mid-April 1945, and the first active group in mid-May. Both targets were exceeded by two weeks. On 26 February the first Junkers-built He 162 was

Above left: The day after the Oranienburg aircraft was rolled out the Marienehe factory produced its first He 162 Volksjäger.

Left: The 'Languste' underground factory at Mödling near Vienna as it is today.

Above: Eleven undamaged Volksjägers (AM 58 to 68) were taken to England after the war or distributed among the Allies.

Right: This He 162 shows all the Gruppe emblems of Jagdgeschwader 1.

Above: Einsatzgruppe I./JG 1 was formed from I. and II./JG 1 in 1945 at Leck.

Left: An He 162 A-2 discovered in a south German scrapyard.

Rocket Aircraft

Above: Four Bachem Natters were captured at St Leonhard in Austria in May 1945.

Right: An aircraft in service with JG 400 at Brandis. On 14 April 1945, two days before their capture by enemy troops, almost all Me 163s were blown up.

Messerschmitt Me 163

The Me 163 B rocket-powered fighter was a cantilever tailless mid-wing monoplane of mixed construction with jettisonable undercarriage and retractable landing skids and tailwheel. The fuselage was a circular cross-section monocoque of overlapping, flush-riveted duralumin panels. They were attached to an armoured nose-cone which also served as ballast in keeping the centre of gravity forward. The single-seat cockpit had an armoured glass canopy and armour plating. The aircraft was powered by a Walter R II 211 (HWK 109-509) liquid-fuelled rocket engine. The two fuels were respectively 'C-Stoff' (methanol, hydrazine hydrate, and water with traces of sodium cuprocyanide as a catalyst) and 'T-Stoff' (hydrogen peroxide). The C-Stoff fuel tanks were located in the wings; the unarmoured fuel tank for T-Stoff

was immediately behind the pilot. The wing had fixed slats and landing flaps, with the trim controls mounted outboard and inboard on the wing trailing edge. The ailerons also served as elevators. Radio equipment consisted of FuG 16 ZE and FuG 25.

As early as 1941 design work for a new rocket-powered fighter with a more powerful engine than the Me 163 A, higher fuel capacity, and a modified wing and fuselage was already at an advanced stage. The project description was issued by the Air Ministry on 22 September 1941. At the same time the Walter factory at Kiel and BMW at Berlin-Spandau were both given the order to produce a more powerful rocket engine.

Construction of the Me 163 B began in the autumn of 1941. The prototype was to be built by Messerschmitt at Augsburg and 68

Left: The first Messerschmitt Me 163 carried the designation AV4 ('KE+SW') and had its first towed test flight on 13 February 1941.

Above: After an exhibition at Peenemünde on 25 August 1942, the Me 163 AV5 was burnt out.

further aircraft at Regensburg. From the Me 163 B V 23, engine installation was done by Klemm at Böblingen, who were also responsible for making all modifications and improvements which occurred during production. On 26 June 1942 the Me 163 B V 1 began unpowered towed test flights. By mid-1943, due to the lack of a functional HWK 509-109 engine, the R II 203 rocket engine of the Me 163 A was used. Later the engine originally intended became available in larger quantities and in reasonably reliable condition. By early 1944 series production of the Me 163 B was well under way. When production ended in January 1945, a total of 364 Me 163 B had been built.

In February 1944 the OKL gave the order to equip the first Jagdgruppe with Me 163 rocket aircraft; this was Jagdgruppe 400. It was recruited from Erprobungskommando 16, which had been stationed at Bad Zwischenahn and had the responsibility for testing the Me 163. Some weeks later the Jagdgruppe was

moved to Wittmundhafen, where a second Staffel was formed. In May 1944 the unit had thirteen rocket fighters, of which only one aircraft was serviceable; the remaining machines were used only for armament testing.

After several air battles against Allied bombers, the build-up of JGr 400 went ahead rapidly. On 31 July 1944 the staff and three squadrons of the group were established. The last of these were based at Stargard. Ergänzungsstaffel 400 with nine Me 163 Bs and some Bf 110s used as tugs was based at Udetfeld. In addition, the establishment of a fourth group with six squadrons and a towing squadron began at Kölleda.

In the late summer of 1944 the first and second squadrons of Jagdgruppe 400 were located at Brandis. There, both squadrons were merged, and Jagdgruppe 400 was expanded to become Jagdgeschwader 400. On 12 November 1944 came the order for a second Gruppe of JG 400, made up of the 3rd and 4th squadrons. Also, the Ergänzungsstaffel, which

meanwhile had been based at Lechfeld, was transformed into an Ergänzungsgruppe. There was also the V.(Ergänzungs)/JG 2 with the 13th to 15th squadrons, which was made up of parts of EK 16; based at Sprottau, it was used for pilot training. In December 1944, JG 400, equipped with 109 Me 163 Bs, was located not only at Brandis but also at bases in Leuna, Pölitz, and Heydebreck.

In April 1945, I./JG 400 had 32 Me 163 Bs and the second Gruppe had about thirteen aircraft. On 7 March the Staff of JG 400, and on 19 April its first and second Gruppen, were dissolved by the OKL. By now replacement by the Me 263 was not possible.

Summary of Me 163 B

Me 163 B-0 V 1 to V 70
latest equipment and modifications from all production series
Engine: HWK 109-509 A
Armament: 2 MG 151/20s to Me 163 BV 45
2 MK 108s from Me 163 BV 46
Radio: FuG 25a and Fug 16 ZE
Me 163 B-0/R1 20 aircraft as Me 163 B-0
Engine: HWK 109-509 A
Armament: 2 MK 108s
Radio: FuG 25a and FuG 16 ZE
Me 163 B-0/R2 30 aircraft as Me 163 B-0, but with the mass-produced wing of the Me 163 B-1
Engine: HWK 109-509 A
Armament: 2 MK 108s

Radio: FuG 25a and FuG 16 ZE
Me 163 B-1/R1 70 aircraft, forward fuselage of the Me 163 B-0, tail section of Me 163 B-1, but with tailplane and rudder, mass-produced wing of the Me 163 B-1
Engine: HWK 109-509 A (with cruise chamber)
Armament: 2 MK 108s
Radio: FuG 25a and FuG 16 ZY
Me 163 B-1 approx. 390 aircraft mass-produced with built-in cruise chamber
Engine: HWK 109-509 A (with cruise chamber)
Armament: 2 MK 108s
Radio: FuG 25a and FuG 16 ZY
Me 163 B-2 Design of whole airframe according to mass-produced requirements of the Me 163 B-0 (without cruise chamber)
Engine: HWK 109-509 A (without cruise chamber)
Armament: 2 MK 108s
Radio: FuG 25a and FuG 16 ZY
Me 163 C-1 Further development of Me 163 B with cranked wings
Engine: HWK 109-509 A (with cruise chamber)
Armament: 2 MK 103s (wing transition)
2 MK 108s (fuselage)
Radio: FuG 25a and FuG 16 ZY

Note that the data given here includes planned production at 23 March 1944 and therefore differs from the number of aircraft produced.

Above: The Me 163 BV21 (Works No 163 10030, 'VA+SS') flew for the first time with a live engine on 24 June 1943. The test machine was used mainly for landing gear and engine power trials.

Right: The cockpit of an Me 163 B-1.

Right: The Me 163 B-1's sprung landing skid.

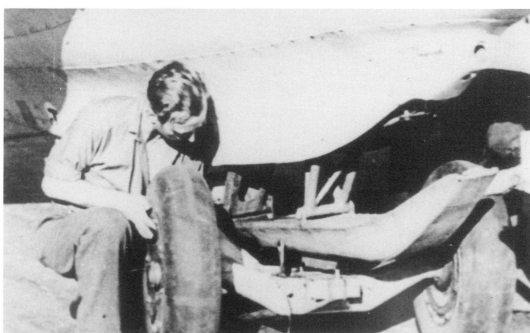

Left: The hydraulically retractable tail-wheel of the Me 163 B-1.

Left: Test run of an Me 163 B-1 by I./JG 400.

Left: For the Me 163 a special vehicle, the 'Scheuch-Schlepper', was developed.

Right: A model of the Ju 248 (Me 236 A-1) in the wind tunnel at the Junkers works at Dessau, remains of which may still be seen today.

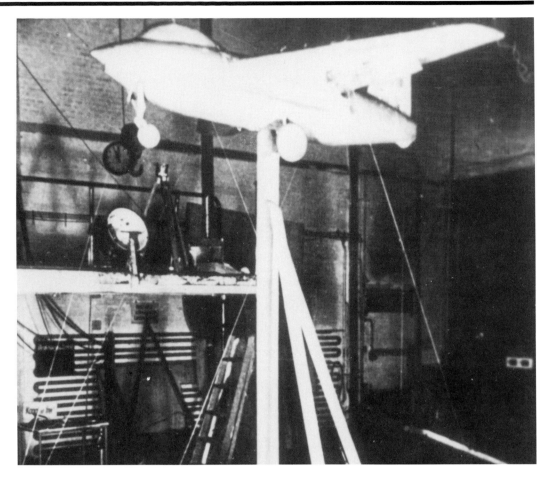

Right: Cockpit mock-up of the planned Ju 248 A-1.

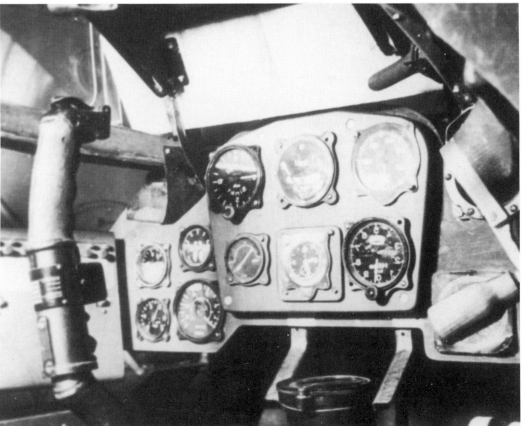

Bachem Ba 349

The Bachem Ba 349 was evolved from an original concept which was submitted to the Air Ministry. During the summer of 1944 Erich Bachem and Willy Fiedler co-operated on a project for a single-seat fighter with a very high rate of climb. One of the basic requirements was a jettisonable trolley undercarriage. Hans Jordanoff, a colleague of Bachem, eventually decided to bring the idea to the attention of the Air Ministry. In addition to the Head of OKL TLR, the design was simultaneously brought to the attention of the SS Fuhrungshauptamt in 1944.

The Bachem was intended to be powered by a HWK 109-509 A-2 liquid-fuelled rocket engine, plus four solid-fuel rockets for take-off from a ramp. Because of the danger of explosion involved in the use of special fuel, Bachem envisaged that the pilot and airframe would land separately by parachute. This meant that the pilot would only have to be trained to fly and shoot; thus the lengthy training in landing and take-off could be dispensed with. After the end of the mission only the armament and the cabin would be lost.

The armament of the 5.72m-long interceptor consisted of two MK 108 cannon and 24 spin-stabilized 'Föhn' rockets, later increased to 48. After reaching its maximum altitude of 12,000m, the 1,700kg Ba 349 reached an average speed of 800km/h. The operational radius was a mere 20km, which required very accurate fighter direction. For this reason the BP 20 (as the type was originally designated) was rightly known as a 'manned anti-aircraft rocket'.

In September 1944 the Air Ministry ordered fifteen prototypes and designated the project Ba 349 in the fighter production programme. After that, full production followed in all building groups. In December 1944 the Ba 349 M-1 was completed with a launch trolley and the M-2 and M-3 with a

Left: An unmanned Bachem BP 20 'Natter' on the launching pad at Heuberg.

Above: Vertical launch of the BP 20 M17 from the 12.5m high launch pad.

Above right: Model of a Ba 349 with a R4M honeycomb, which could take 24 of these projectiles.

Right: Tests of the solid fuel auxiliary launch rockets at the Bachem works at Waldsee.

fixed undercarriage which had been modified from a Klemm Kl 35. This allowed the possibility of towed trials to determine flying characteristics. That month the first HWK 105-509 A-1 engine was installed at Waldsee and the first towed flight was made with the Ba 349 M-3 at Neuburg-Donau. At the end of December 1944 the first successful unmanned vertical launch was made at Heuberg bei Stetten, after an initial failure. Simultaneously, up to the end of January 1945, wind-tunnel testing on a small scale model was being carried out at the DVL.

On 14 February 1945 the Ba 349 M-8 made a towed test flight which also included the first free flight without power. A week later the first fully realistic vertical take-off test of a powered machine, including a test separation, took place. The pilot dummy and the tail section came down safely to earth by parachute. On 1 March the Ba 349 M-23 faced its first take-off. It was intended to be the first manned vertical take-off. The pilot, Lothar Sieber, lost his life.

Up to the end of March several unmanned vertical take-offs followed. On the 20th of that month, however, General Dornberger removed the Ba 349 from the test programme. Also the

SS showed no further interest, since no fuel for use for this kind of aircraft was available. Nevertheless, the Ba 349 continued to be built at Waldsee and Nabern/Teck. Some 35 aircraft were produced. From April 1945 the transfer of the Bachem factory to Bad Wörrishofen took place, where an advance command remained for only a short time. Together with five production models, important construction details, solid fuel rockets, and replacement components, some Bachem workers were captured by Americans at St Leonhard in Austria at the beginning of May.

Top, left and right: A total of 34 Natters were built or were in preparation before the end of the war.

Above centre: Launch preparations at Heuberg. The first unmanned launch (M7) took place on 18 December 1944, with the first manned launch (M23) on 1 March 1945.

Above: Wooden mock-up of a series type of Ba 349 A-1 with R4M armament.

Above: One of the fast He 70 light bombers and reconnaissance aircraft used during the Spanish Civil War.

Above: Full-scale mock-up of the Arado Ar 240 V-11. Clearly visible are the pressurized cockpit and MG 151/20 mounted at the side of the fuselage.

Below: For the Ar 240 heavy fighter a remote-controlled MG 131 and an MG 151 were fitted as defensive armament.

Above: The Arado Ar 234 B-2 bomber, construction of which began in September 1944 at Landeshut/Schlesien, was the forerunner of the Ar 234 B-2/N auxiliary night fighter.

Below: Model of the Ar 234 C-5. From November 1944, a night fighter version (Ar 234 C-5/N) was wind-tunnel tested.

Left: The Me 262 A-1a (V056) was the test-bed for all proposed night fighter versions of the famous jet fighter.

Left: Herbert Dieks, Wolfgang Heinemann, Klaus Metzner and Hermann Neninger in front of the Lippisch DM 1 glider discovered at Prien am Chiemsee. The DM 1 was intended to test the unusual delta configuration for the planned jet and rocket-powered fighters.

Left: The DM 1 at Prien awaiting transport to the USA in the summer of 1945.

Above: Me 262 A-1a at Messerschmitt's airfield at Lager Lechfeld.   **Below:** An Fw 190 fighter bomber being prepared for offensive action.

This photo of three Do 17 E-1s
with MG 15s in their noses was
taken during training in Bavaria.

Above: This Ju 88 A-4 was operated together with Ju 88 D-1 and D-5 by Aufklärungsgruppe 14.

Below: In central Germany several production sites were situated in tunnels and other facilities far away from Allied bombs.

Part Two
BOMBERS

Above: The He 111 H-11 and H-16 undertook a new role during the second part of the Russian campaign. More and more He 111s were used as transports.

Below: This He 111 H-4 was operated by KG 27 over Russia in 1942.

Introduction

From its origins in the First World War, the bomber underwent rapid development. The 'flying teachests' of the early war years, with their makeshift bombing equipment, became commercial airliners with four or more engines of respectable power and imposing dimensions for their time.

The Treaty of Versailles did not succeed in curbing the enthusiasm of Germany's aircraft builders. In secret, a new Luftwaffe, larger and more powerful than the old one, came into existence. Using all sorts of subterfuge, and with the help of the USSR and other neutral states, the Reichswehr set about creating newer, more up-to-date aircraft.

The expansion of German military aircraft construction in the 1930s led, despite all planning directives, to a multiplicity of different models with hundreds of production series and thousands of modifications. From basic models such as the Ju 52 K and the Ju 86, types such as the Ju 88, He 111, and Do 217 were developed, which would be taken over by 'Bomber A'and 'Bomber B', before moving to the era of the jet aircraft.

Furthermore, adding to the interest of a chronology such as this, there were a large number of different designs and projects, only a few of which ever reached the flying prototype stage. For reasons of space, it is only possible to show a limited selection of bombers, the introduction of which by the Luftwaffe was doomed to failure for many reasons.

The documentation also shows that supplies to the German air force, in contrast to those of the Allies, were always pushed to the limit. Production capacity, raw materials, and labour were never sufficient. A war against half of the world must inevitably overtax the capabilities of a single country such as Germany. Only the bureaucrats of the Reichsluftfahrtministerium (RLM) seemed not to notice that the world was in flames around them, and

pursued their plans even when allied troops had crossed the Rhine and the Red Army stood at the Oder.

The change from piston-engined to jet bombers was far from easy. The new technology was misjudged by both the Party and the Luftwaffe leadership. Göring's maxim: "When I order, technology responds," had immense status in the Third Reich. Hitler's involvement in current events, along with unqualified leadership personnel, hindered rather than accelerated development. Effective authority was blocked, and decisions were taken that sometimes arose more from chance than from anything else.

Furthermore, the development of almost all of the German bombers was hindered by the low power of the available aero-engines. The fatal belief that it was possible to proceed without suitable materials led to many routes being ignored, while others were followed erroneously for years in the interests of the blitzkrieg. The results, which only became apparent between 1943 and 1945, were seen in an ever more serious shortfall in materials. Airframes assembled in the forests should serve as a sufficient example of this. It was, and is, astounding that, under such limiting conditions, aircraft such as the Fw 190, Me 262 and He 162 could be produced at all.

By the end of the war a technology of cellular airframe construction had been established. Aerodynamics in the sphere of bomber development had reached a stage that would not be surpassed until well into the 1950s.

In the compilation of this book, the authors wish to thank the following for their invaluable assistance: U. Balke, P. Zollner (BMW), R. Chapman, E. Creek and the Air Force Archive, the German Museum at Munich and especially Dipl Ing Heinzerling, A.Krüger, Dr Heinrichs and Limmer, and also H.-P. Dabrowski, K. Francella, Dr Wustrak, J.

INTRODUCTION

Prowan and Mr Meier of Frankfurt am Main Airport AG, P.K. Herrendorf, J. Bekker, H. Brieke, S. Brozutzki, H. Berresheim of Ada Opel AG, B. Filley, and D. Herwig of the Deutschen Studienbüro für Luftfahrt (German Aeronautical Design Office), Dr A. Hiller, K. Junges, N. Arena, Dipl-Karl Kössler, H. Kruse, B. Lange and H. J. Meier, H. Roosenboom, as well as E. Götsch and H. Pause of the Henschel Werken GmbH (MBB). Thanks are also due to R.P. Lutz Jr, B. Kudlicka, F. Marshall, J. Menke, Th. Mohr, F. Müller-Romminger, J.P. Silva, H. Sander, H. Scheibert, G. Schlaug, and Messrs. Mikesh and S.E. Ewing as well as their team at the National Air and Space Museum in Washington, DC, H.J. Nowarra (+), P. Petrick, W. Pervesler, and Dr A. Price. Invaluable help was also given by G. Sengfelder, W. Radinger, S. Ranson and the Factory Archive of DASA, F. Selinger, H. Schliephake, Ch. Regel, H. Riedinger of Siemens AG in Munich, R. Smith, K. Soppa, H.-H. Stapfer, F. Trenkle and S. Neitzel. For their helpful support we are also grateful to Frau Müller of the Wehrbereichsbibliothek IV (Military Library) at Mainz, the Zentralbibliothek der Bundeswehr (Central Army Library) at Dresden, the staff of the Bundesarchiv (National Archives) at Koblenz, especially Dr Hofmann, Fr Pfeffer and Mr Nilges. Thanks are also due to the Bundesarchiv at Freiburg, as well as to the Militärgeschichtlichen Forschungsamt (Military Research Establishment) and especially to K. H. Heinkel and his colleagues for great support and unlimited help.

Mainz/Hochheim, October 1993
Manfred Griehl, Joachim Dressel

Right: This He 111 H-3 of KG 100 was first used for the night bombing of Britain and later served in the Mediterranean area.

Below: This photograph was taken in action on 13 August 1940 by KG 27, which was stationed at Tours, Dinard, and Rheims.

Early Bombers

Left: The Do K3 was designed as an auxiliary bomber as well as a commercial airliner; its first flight took place on 17 August 1931.

Below left: The Do N medium bomber flew for the first time on 19 June 1926, and was manufactured under licence by Kawasaki of Japan as the Ka 87.

Right: The Do P was introduced on 31 March 1930, powered by four 500hp Bristol Jupiter engines.

Below: The flying weight of the Do P was 12,000kg and its speed was 210km/h.

Improvised Bombers

The build-up of the German bomber force began about 1925 under various forms of subterfuge, often with the help of neighbouring countries. In the summer of 1928 a Rohrbach Ro VIII Mb, a military version of the Ro VIII Roland three-engined commercial aircraft, was tested at Lipetsk as an 'improvised bomber'. In comparison, the Junkers G 24ge was better. With their new equipment, these commercial aircraft were just as fast in the bomber role. A G 24 was tested at Adlershof with a rack for three 300kg or twelve 50kg bombs. Its defensive armament consisted of a single MG 08/15 machine gun in the top of the fuselage.

For the second test programme at Lipetsk, Rohrbach proposed its Ro XII Roka aircraft.

The Ro XII was fitted with racks to enable it to carry three 300kg bombs under the fuselage and two clusters of five 50kg anti-personnel bombs under the wing roots. The relocation of the 50kg bombs in a shallow hollow in the fuselage, with the possibility of loading from a bomb carrier brought underneath the fuselage, was also tested.

In 1925 the Junkers K 30 was developed as an operational aircraft from the G 23 and G 24 commercial transports. Although the Reichswehr showed no interest, Junkers sold 34 of these aircraft to Chile, Spain, Yugoslavia and the USSR between 1925 and 1935. These bombers and long-distance reconnaissance aircraft, which were built in Sweden, could be fitted with wheel undercarriage, skis, or floats.

Below: The Do Y w
ered by Bristol Jupi
Testing of the three
bomber began on
1931.

Right: In 1933 the
the first Do Y test
mercial use was p
was not carried ou

At the end of 1929 a request for tender was issued for a medium night bomber ('Minabo') and long-range reconnaissance aircraft in two series. Junkers refused to develop a corresponding aircraft, but instead offered the K 30 in modified form as a night bomber. The order therefore went to Dornier for its Do-F, which later became the Do 11. This aircraft had a wing span of 26.6m and a length of 18.2m. For its first flight, at Altenrhein on 17 January 1931, it was powered by three Bristol Jupiter VI engines driving two-bladed wooden propellers. Later these were replaced by Gnome et Rhone Jupiter VI 9 engines of 625hp (460kW) take-off power. Its maximum speed was about 300km/h and range about 1,500km. Armament comprised ring-mounted double machine guns on the nose and upper rear fuselage, and a single pivot-mounted ventral machine gun. The maximum bomb load was 1,200kg.

Up to 1932 Dornier produced three of these medium bombers, but the Reichswehr showed no interest because twin-engined aircraft were more economic. In 1937 the aircraft, now designated Do 15, was sold to Yugoslavia.

Dornier Do 11

The order for the Do-F night bomber (later the Do 11) was raised by the Reichsverkehrministerium (RVM) as a cargo and postal aircraft. The first flight of this twin-engined shoulder-wing aircraft, produced at Altenrhein, took place on 7 May 1932. After several test flights for the Reichsverband der deutschen Luftfahrtindustrie (RdL), it underwent technical and tactical testing at Lipetsk the same year. As the first bomber, it was intended to carry the new SC bombs, and it could take either six vertically-mounted magazines containing a total of 30 50kg bombs, or 120 10kg bombs on a special type of bomb rack.

This aircraft, designated Do 11 in its military form, was satisfactory as far as power was concerned, but suffered from poor flying quali-

ties. Moreover, the manually assembled airframe was found to be too weak, which resulted in wing vibration and fuselage deformation.

From 1932 mass production of the Do 11 C began at Friedrichshafen, with Siemens Sh 22 B-2 engines replacing the Siemens Jupiter VI. This variant served mainly as a trainer for bomber crews, and had covered gun positions and no glazing in the nose.

The Do 11 D had a retractable undercarriage, a new type of rudder control, and additional fins under the tailplane. Reducing the span from 28m to 26.3m failed to alleviate wing vibration because the problem lay in the weak fuselage. Of 150 ordered only 76 were delivered.

Below: Officially, the Do 11 D was a mail and freight carrier. The airframe however, had provision for carrying armament.

Right: So many problems were experienced with the retractable undercarriage of the Do 11 that the designers later reverted to a fixed undercarriage.

Dornier Do 13 and Do 23

In February 1933 the Dornier Do 13 A was introduced as a development of the Do 11. It had a rigid, fabric-covered fuselage and the same wingspan, 28m, as the Do 11 C, but used the Junkers double-wing flaps and ailerons and the Siemens Jupiter VI engine, later replaced by the more powerful BMW VI 7.3 ZU when it went into mass production. After a few problems had been overcome, production began in earnest.

Since it did not prove to be a suitable alternative, Dornier tried every possible improvement to the fuselage and wings to rescue the design. In September 1934 tests began on the much-modified aircraft, now designated Do 23 F.

Further strengthening resulted in the Do 23 G production version, which, however, had a higher flying weight. Up to 1936 240 were produced by Dornier at Manzell and Wismar, and by Henschel and the Hamburger Flugzeugbau. This all-metal aircraft was replaced as the standard bomber of the Luftwaffe by the Junkers Ju 86.

Left: Most Do 23 Fs were committed to training after the introduction of the Ju 86.

Below left: The first flight of the Do 23 F took place on 1 September 1934. It was powered by two BMW VI U in-line engines.

Right: The Do 23 was armed with three MG 15s, and a simple bomb sight was located in the nose.

Left: The Ju K 43 'Bolivar' was based on the Ju W 34, and was built in 1930 as an auxiliary bomber for export.

Left: The Ju S 36 was tested in the autumn of 1927 in Sweden. In the background a Ju K 39 can be seen.

Left: The Ju K 39 (Ju A 32) was designed as a light bomber or three-seat reconnaissance aircraft.

Left: As an alternative to floats, the He 59 was fitted with a faired undercarriage for test purposes.

Junkers Ju 52 K

Below: Officially, the Ju 52 K was described as a bomber, although it was more of a solution to an embarrassment, since suitable aircraft were not available initially.

Since the problems with the Do 11 meant that no great numbers would be built in the foreseeable future, Junkers received an order to convert the Ju 52 three-engined airliner into an improvised bomber. The Junkers works at Dessau began conversion of the first Ju 52/3m in 1934. The Auxiliary Bomber Group 1, founded in January of the same year under the guise of a Lufthansa inspectorate, was equipped in March 1934 with three Do 11s and 24 Ju 52/3ms. From the middle of 1934 mass production of the Ju 52/3m began. The basic airframe was the same as that of the civilian version, and its armament consisted of one

movable dorsal MG 15 machine gun on the rear fuselage and another in a retractable 'dustbin' in the cabin floor. The bomb load was 1,500kg.

At this time Bomber Group (KG) 154 was established, and on 15 March 1936 it was followed by KG 152. These were renamed KG 1 'Hindenburg' on 1 May 1939. They were followed by KG 253, equipped with Do 23s and Ju 86s, and by KG 155 in the early part of 1937. It was intended to equip this last group solely with the Do 17 E, but it eventually also received Ju 52/3ms. In August and September 1938 the Staff and I./KG 252 were

established at Cottbus, and II./KG 252 was created as a second group from the existing IV./KG 153.

Because of its ruggedness, the Ju 52 took on a significance far in excess of that initially envisaged during the Luftwaffe's formative years. From the end of 1935 up to the introduction of the He 111 and Ju 86 medium bombers, almost two-thirds of the operational aircraft of the Luftwaffe bomber force were Ju 52/3ms. In all, 760 were delivered.

The Ju 52/3m g3e could also be used as a night bomber. It had improved radio direction-finding equipment and a better bomb-release mechanism. An export version, the Ju 52/3m g4e, had the same powerplant and equipment, and differed only in having a tailwheel instead of the earlier skid. Most examples of this variant were taken over by the Luftwaffe, and only a few went abroad. The Ju 52 first saw active service as a transport and bomber in the Spanish Civil War. Before the beginning of the Second World War the majority of the remaining Ju 52 auxiliary bombers were reconverted to serve in the transport role by removal of their lower gun mountings.

Left: The Ju 52 was fitted with a fixed wing-mounted MG 17 for test purposes.

Left: A retractable turret with a D 51 'Argus' rotary mount and Rheinmetall MG 15 machine gun served as rear defensive armament for the Ju 52 K.

Junkers Ju 86

The Junkers Ju 86 was also introduced into combat in Spain, having appeared as a medium bomber of modern design at the beginning of 1934. Competing designs had been produced by Dornier and Heinkel. At the same time, Luft Hansa was seeking a fast commercial aircraft to carry up to ten passengers. Because of its experience in the design of heavy-oil engines, Junkers gave its design the Jumo 205 diesel engine.

On 4 November 1934 the first prototype, originally designated Ju 86abl and later Ju 86 V 1, made its maiden flight. Because the Jumo 205 was not yet available, it was powered by two Siemens SAM 22 nine-cylinder radial engines driving two-bladed wooden propellers. During the test flight problems were experienced with control responses, the aircraft tending to yaw. While it was undergoing modification the Ju 86 V 1 was fitted with its dorsal and ventral gun positions. The second prototype, which, like the fourth test model, was equipped as a commercial aircraft, flew for the first time on 22 March 1935. The third prototype, the Ju 86cb, had a fully-glazed nose with an MG 15 machine gun on a rotary mount. The Ju 86 V 5, which first flew in August 1935, had larger wings, a tailwheel in place of a skid, improved cooling, modified cockpit glazing, and a modified retractable ventral turret.

Construction of the zero series began at the end of 1935. This consisted of seven commercial aircraft and thirteen bombers designated Ju 86 A-0 and powered by the Jumo 205

Below: This Ju 86 A-1 flew with Bomber Group K/88 of the Condor Legion during the Spanish Civil War.

C engine. In February 1936 the Luftwaffe took charge of these machines for testing. Delivery of the A-1 series followed in the early summer of 1936, and was based on fifteen test models powered by the Jumo 205 C-4. Despite improved wings, the yaw stability of the Ju 86 A was never remarkable.

One aircraft was taken from the zero series, given the designation Ju 86 V 6, and used for stability testing. One solution was found to be a wedge-shaped rearwards extension of the fuselage. With this modification and increased fuel tankage, the Ju 86 D-1 entered production in the late summer of 1936. As its defensive armament this variant had three movable MG 15 machine guns, and it could carry up to sixteen SC 50 bombs in the bomb bay. This all-metal, smooth-skinned, low-wing aircraft had a maximum speed of 325km/h at 3,000m. With a full bomb load it had a range of 550km at a cruising speed of 235km/h.

At the time the Ju 86 D-1 went into series production the disadvantages of the diesel engine were already apparent. Its slow reaction to changes in power requirement were especially unsuitable for military conditions, and it was also subject to failure through overheating and piston seizing. The use of four Ju 86 Ds in the Spanish Civil War emphasized these tactical disadvantages. In civilian operations, when the aircraft was flown at constant speeds, the economy and durability of the Jumo 205 was a very positive benefit.

Above: Swearing-in of Luftwaffe airmen at Fliegerhorst Lechfeld. A Ju 86 E-2 stands next to the fire station.

Right: This matched pair consists of a Ju 86 A-1 and D-1 of KG 253 in flight on National Party Day, 1936.

Owing to the unfavourable experiences with diesel engines, the first of the Ju 86 D-1 series was experimentally fitted by BMW with the American Pratt & Whitney Hornet engine. In early 1937 this aircraft, now designated Ju 86 V 9, was subjected to intensive flight testing at Rechlin. As a result, Junkers decided that the next Ju 86 variant should be powered by the BMW 132 F injection engine. Aircraft of this new series, designated Ju 86 E-1, were delivered to the Luftwaffe from the late summer of 1937. After 30 aircraft of this series had been built, the 864hp (636kW) BMW 132 N was adopted and the designation changed to Ju 86 E-2.

In 1938 the Ju 86 V 10, a Ju 86 E-1 with fully glazed nose and a more compact cockpit mounted further forward, was tested at Rechlin. This type went into production with the altered nose in early 1938 as the Ju 86 G-1, and in the early summer of the same year, after about 40 Ju 86 G-1s had been converted from other models, the Ju 86 was mass-produced.

Left: The Ju 86 D-1 was replaced by the considerably improved G-1 version. An MG 15 was installed in the nose position.

Left: A Ju 86 G-1 after a crash at Prague-Rusin. The type was powered by two BMW 132 N radial engines.

Left: This unarmed Ju 86 G-1 was allocated to a flying school.

Dornier Do 17

In 1932 the Ordnance Department (Heereswaffenamt, HWA) issued development guidelines for the construction of a twin-engined bomber with retractable undercarriage. Dornier was involved in this project, as well as Heinkel, Junkers and a few other — unsuccessful — firms. At Friedrichshafen on the Bodensee, construction of a 'freight aircraft for German State Railways' and a 'high-speed mail plane for Luft Hansa' was begun. Initially using the designation Do 17, the factory began design of the 'mail plane' on 1 August 1932. On 17 March 1933 the go-ahead for construction was given, and a few months later, on 24 May, Erhard Milch gave the green light for the building of two prototypes.

At the end of 1933 the RLM placed development and delivery orders for a 'high-speed commercial aircraft with double tail' (the Ju 86

Below: The fast, stylish Do 17 astounded visitors to the Dübendorfer Flugmeeting.

was originally produced to a DLH requirement), and for a 'freight aircraft with special equipment'— in other words, a bomber.

In April 1934 the Dornier works at Manzell began the project definition. Here the defensive armament and the first designs for the bomb release gear ('special equipment') were discussed. Production of the military version began at Friedrichshafen on 20 May 1934. On 20 November 1934 the Bauaufsicht Luft (BAL) took over the first prototype, and three days later the Do 17 V 1 made its first flight. The second prototype followed on 18 May 1935, and the third, the Do 17 V 3, flew in September 1935 at Rechlin. The V 2 and later the V 4 were used for testing, *inter alia*, a 20mm gun and the MG 15 machine gun.

As a result of the positive outcome of these flying tests, the RLM ordered eleven fur-

ther test models (V 4 - V 14). Prototypes V 6 and V 9 served as high-speed airliners. The Do 17 V 8 was the forerunner of the long-distance reconnaissance version, the Do 17 F-1, and the Do V 11, equipped as a production aircraft, became the F-2 prototype. The Do 17 E-1 was tested with two DB 600 engines, and in 1937 the Do 17s V 15-V 17 appeared with Bramo 323 engines. The succeeding V 18-V 21 had BMW 132 F engines.

At the International Air Show at Düben-dorf (Switzerland) in 1937, the Do 17 MV 1 proved to be the undoubted leader in its class. It was even faster than the Czechoslovakian and French fighters. Likewise, many prizes were won by the Bf 109 and other German air-craft.

The second Dornier Do17 M prototype had Bramo 323 engines, and the third was the initial model for series production. That same year saw the appearance of the reconnaissance version, the Do 17 P, which, together with the F series, was to equip Reconnaissance Groups 10, 11, 14, 22 and 31. Dornier next developed the Do 17 Z, with a modified cockpit, Bramo 323 A-1 engines, and improved fighting capability.

The first prototype of this series (D-ABVD) strongly resembled the planned design of the Do 17 Z-1. The following version, the Do 17 Z-2, differed in having Bramo 323 P Fafnir engines and an increase in bomb load from 500kg to 1,000kg. Up to May 1940, 422 Do 17 Zs flew with Bomber Groups 2, 3, 76 and 77.

The Do 17 Z-3 became the lead aircraft for the bomber force as the 'staff squadron reconnaissance aircraft'. This carried up to five MG 15 guns in the upper turret, Rb 50/30 and Rb 20/30 movie cameras plus Z-3 and Z-5 still cameras, and improved radio equipment. The Do 17 Z-4 was a blind-flying trainer with dual control.

The Do 17 Z-5 carried the same equipment as the Z-3 series. Structurally it was identical to the Z-2, but it had additional emergency ditching equipment in the form of an inflatable dinghy.

The Do 17 Z-6 was a weather reconnaissance aircraft, although it was also built as a prototype. The 'Geier' bomber, or Do 17 Z-8, was never produced. The Z-9 was a prototype with special bomb release equipment and modified delayed-action release gear for use in low-level attack. Finally, the Do 17 Z-7 ('Kauz I') and Do 17 Z-10 ('Kauz II') were attached to NJG 1 as night fighters and, later, to NJG 2 in the same role.

Above: The Do 17 M-1 was an early replacement for the E-1. This aircraft is having its under-carriage tested at the factory before delivery.

Top right: This Do 17 Z-2, a medium-range bomber, was attached to Bomber Squadron KG 2 ('Holzhammer'), which saw action mainly in Western Europe.

Right: The Do 17 Z-3 could carry a bomb load of up to 500kg. An Rb 20/30 was originally fitted in the ventral gun position.

Above: The heavily-armed Do 17 Z-5 was a conversion of the Z-2, and carried inflatable flotation bags for emergency ditchings.

Left: The defensive armament in the 'Kampfkopf' usually consisted of seven MG 15s. This aircraft came down in Italy in 1944.

Dornier Do 215

A direct improvement of the Do 17 Z, the Do 215 was powered by the liquid-cooled Daimler-Benz DB 601 12-cylinder vee engine which developed 1,100hp (810kW).

The Do 215 V 1 (D-AFFY) crashed on its first flight, on 29 October 1938. Flight testing proceeded with the Do 215 V 2, which for the tests was fitted with French Gnome et Rhone engines. The Do 215 V 3 was the forerunner of the A-1 series, with DB 601 A-1 engines. Series production began with the four-seat, long-range-reconnaissance Do 215 B-1. The Do 215 B-2 bomber flew with its defensive armament increased to five MG 15 machine guns, and also had DB 601 A-1 engines.

The Do 215 B-3 was powered by DB 601 Aa engines of 1,175hp (865kW), and the long-

range-reconnaissance Do 215 B-4 was identical apart from its camera equipment. Some export versions of the Do 215 B-2 and B-4 were sold to Hungary, and two Do 215 B-13s entered service with the Soviet Air Force.

With the delivery of the Junkers Ju 88 D-1, the Do 215 B-4 ended its service with 1.(F)/124 and Reconnaissance Group ObdL.

The high-altitude, long-range-reconnaissance Do 215 B-6 appeared only as a single prototype with the DB 601 T engine, designed for a full-power altitude of 9,000m and fitted with two TK 9A turbochargers. The aircraft was intended to have a service ceiling of over 11,000m. As with the Heinkel He 111, problems with the underdeveloped and complex engines reduced its operational usefulness.

Below: A Do 215 B-0 during engine testing over southern Germany.

Left: The Do 215 B-1 was powered by two DB 601 Aa in-line engines. Most examples were used as long-range reconnaissance aircraft.

Left: The Do 215 B-2 was a four-seat medium bomber with six MG 15s as defensive armament.

Standard Bombers

Right: An He 111 H-2 with the 'Knickebein' and 'X-Gerät' radio navigation systems leads aircraft of KG 100 over the North Sea.

Below: A Do 217 E-2 of KG 66 at Montdidier. The aircraft is equipped with a rear attack warning device.

Heinkel He 111 A to F

The prototype Heinkel He 111 a (designated V 1 after the introduction of the standard numbering scheme) took off from Rostock-Marienehe on its maiden flight on 24 February 1935, with Heinkel test pilot Gerhard Nitschke at the controls. From the outset its flying qualities were good and it handled well during landing, but a tendency to drop a wing in the stall necessitated structural modifications. For this reason, both prototypes of the commercial version of the He 111 (V 2 and V 4) had the wingspan reduced to 23m from the 25m of the V 1, while the V 3 and V 5 spanned 22.6m.

The first prototypes were underpowered with 578hp (425kW) BMW VI 6.0 six-cylinder in-line engines, but take-off power was increased to 999hp (735kW) with the advent of the more powerful DB 600 which was fitted to the V 5, which thus became the prototype for

the B-Series. Because of the low engine power available, few A-Series models were built. In the end, however, the He 111 became — after the Ju 52 K — an effective standard bomber.

The first of ten He 111 Bs made its maiden flight at Rechlin in the autumn of 1936. After the elimination of a few small deficiencies in flying characteristics, and some modifications to the military equipment, the RLM ordered 300 He 111 B-1s, and these began to be delivered to bomber squadrons in January 1937. The following series (B-2) had the supercharged DB 600 C 850hp (625kW) or 600 G 952hp (700kW) engine, and began to come off the production lines of the new Heinkel Works at Oranienburg in 1937.

When the DB 600 Ga engine, with a take-off power of 1,047hp (770kW), became available in the summer of 1937, Heinkel used it for

Below: The He 111a (later redesignated He 111 V1) flew for the first time on 24 February 1935 at Marienehe, near Rostock.

Right: This He 111 B-2 was attached to Bomber Group K 88 in Spain, where the type carried the tactical code numbers 25•41 to 25•62.

Below right: The He 111 B-2, powered by twin DB 600 engines, flew for a while with KG 154 before being replaced by the E-1 series.

Left: This He 111 was photographed at Leon in Spain in August 1938, where it served with Bomber Group K 88.

Right: Flight operations at the Oranienburg factory near Berlin. The aircraft are He 111 E-3 medium-range bombers.

Below right: This retired He 111 F-4 with armament removed is seen at the FFS C Flying School at Brunswick.

the He 111 V 9 prototype of the B-type zero series. This aircraft still had the He 111 B-2 cooler which produced a great deal of drag.

The D-1 Series entered production in the autumn of 1937 in the Heinkel factories at Marienehe and Oranienburg and in the Dornier works at Wismar without the promised DB 600 engine, which was reserved for the Messerschmitt Bf 109 and 110. Heinkel anticipated the problem and attempted to find a solution by using Jumo engines. The He 111 V 6 was tested with two Jumo 210 G engines in the summer of 1937, but they were not powerful enough. However, the improved 999hp (735kW) Jumo 211 A-1 gave satisfactory results, so the RLM cancelled the D-series and ordered the design of the He 111 E. The pre-series prototype (V 10) was taken from the He 111 D-0 series and was delivered in January 1938. In February the first E-1 came off the production line, and it went into service with K/88 of the Condor Legion in Spain in March 1938.

The main series began with the He 111 E-3, with a few modifications in equipment. External bomb racks were fitted to the E-4, and at the same time a minor series, the He 111 E-5, given increased range by fitting additional fuel tanks in the port side of the bomb bay, was produced.

Because the elliptical wing planform had caused manufacturing problems, a new shape, with a straight leading edge, was introduced, and resulted in the creation of the F-1 series at the end of 1937. This series, powered by the Jumo 211 A-3, went entirely to Turkey. A production batch of 40 He 111 F-4s, which corresponded to the E-4 but lacked the additional fuel tanks, went into service with the Luftwaffe in the summer of 1938.

The He 111 J was intended as a torpedo bomber, and was powered by the DB 600. It was fitted with two external racks each carrying a torpedo, but had no bomb bay. In mid-1938 the RLM issued an order for the bomb bay to be retrofitted, and this variant was then known as the He 111 J-1, although it was identical to the F-4 apart from its powerplant.

Problems with pilot visibility led Heinkel to begin studies of a new system of cockpit glazing in 1937. Consequently, the V-8 series appeared in January 1938 with a semi-circular canopy with all-round visibility and a built-in asymmetric Ikaria nose mounting for an MG 15 machine gun. This redesign reduced the length of the aircraft by 1.1m. The V-7 followed in early 1938, and served as the prototype for a new trapezoidal wing-form as well as for the new cockpit design. To improve aerodynamics still further, the retractable turret was replaced by a faired-in ventral gondola. Additionally, the semi-open dorsal gun position was now fully glazed. Powered by the larger DB 601 Aa engine of 1168hp (860kW) take-off power, examples of this new variant were delivered to Marienehe in the autumn of 1938 as pre-series aircraft with the designation He 111 P-0. In the winter of 1938/39 the type began to be produced under licence by Arado at Warnemünde and Dornier at Wismar as the

He 111 P, and the first P-1 went into service with the Luftwaffe in early 1939. At 5,000m the bomber had a maximum speed of 475km/h and a cruising speed of 370km/h. This was reduced to 300km/h with the full 2,000kg bomb load. In May 1939 improved radio equipment was fitted to the He 111 P-2. However, the P-2s available at the beginning of the war were later, like the He 111 P-4, fitted with stronger armour, two additional MG 15s in the cabin side windows, and two external bomb racks.

The He 111 P-6, powered by the DB 601 N engine, was the last of the P-series. In the summer of 1940 the RLM abandoned the He 111 P in favour of the He 111 H, and some of the He 111 P-6s in service were redesignated He 111 P-6/R2 and used as heavy glider tugs. Ten P-6s were delivered to the Hungarian air force for long-range reconnaissance.

Heinkel He 111 H

Because of uncertainty regarding the delivery of DB 601 engines (which, it had been announced, were intended for fighter production), Heinkel began tests with the Jumo 211 A in the seventh prototype, which was now designated He 111 V 19. The aircraft first flew in January 1939 and became the prototype for the He 111 H.

The H-series which went into service resembled the He 111 P-2 apart from their 1,010hp (743kW) Jumo 211 A-1 engines. At the beginning of the war, this series began to be replaced by the H-2 with the more powerful 1,100hp (809kW) Jumo 211 A-3 engine.

A count made on 2 September 1939 revealed that the Luftwaffe had 787 He 111s in service. This included approximately 400 He 111 H-1s and H-2s which had been produced in a mere four months. Production of the main series, the He 111 H-3 powered by the 1,200hp (880kW) Jumo 211 D-1, began in November 1939.

At the end of 1940 a smaller production series of He 111 H-4s followed, these being powered by the Jumo 211 D-1 and H-1. In this variant the internal fuselage bomb load was limited to four 250kg bombs, but it could also carry individual loads up to 1,800kg on the

Below: The He 111 J-1 was very similar to the F-4 but was powered by two DB 600 in-line engines.

external bomb racks. A smaller batch of H-5s followed in February 1941; these were identical to the H-4s apart from their heavier defensive armament.

The H-6 represented a considerable all-round improvement, beginning with the improved Jumo 211 F-1 engine of 1,350hp (990kW). The defensive armament was upgraded, with one MG-FF in the nose and one MG 15 in the ventral turret, plus a heavy MG 17 in the tail and MG 15s in the cabin side windows. The internal bomb bay for four ESAC 250/IX was retained, but extra bomb racks capable of carrying bombs or torpedoes up to 2,000kg (2 ETC 2000/XII A or PVC 1006) were fitted. The He 111 Z-1 'Zwilling' or Twin, a twin-fuselaged, five-engined combination of two H-6 aircraft, was tried in mid-1942 as a tug for the Messerschmitt Me 321 heavy glider. There was also a design project for a long-range bomber (Z-2), and the Z-3, a long-range-reconnaissance version based on the Z-1. The He 111 H-7 was a night bomber based on H-6 and with a reduced defensive armament.

About 30 H-3 and H-5 aircraft powered by the Jumo 211 D were fitted with barrage balloon cable-cutting equipment in the form of a cutter mounted forward of the engines and cockpit, and were designated H-8. However, the extra weight and the change in weight distribution made this aircraft very difficult to fly. Because of the lack of power the majority of the remaining He 111 H-8 aircraft were converted to tugs and redesignated He 111 H-8/R2.

Both the H-9 and H-10 were rebuilt He 111 H-1 and H-2 models. They were fitted with dual controls and were used as training aircraft.

With the advent of the H-11, the Luftwaffe became equipped with a relatively powerful medium-range bomber with heavier armour and defensive armament. The dorsal gun position was fully enclosed and given armoured glazing and a WL 131 AL roller-mount for an MG 131 machine gun. The single MG 18 in the ventral turret was replaced by two MG 81s, and the side-mounted MG 15s were relpaced by MG 81 Z guns. With these modifications the H-11 was given the designation He 111 H-11/R1, and the R2 versions were fitted with tow couplings.

Below: With the introduction of the H series (an He 111 H-1 is shown here), a considerable increase in performance and payload became available.

At the beginning of 1943 small numbers of the H-12 series were delivered as trainers or for test work with the Hs 293A glider bomb. A 'Kehl III' radio-control transmitter was located in the dorsal gun position, and the flight observer controlled the Hs 293 from the nose turret. According to factory information, the ventral turret of the H-12 was fitted with one MG 81Z and one MG 15.

The He 111 H-14 was an H-3 but was armed similarly to the He 111 H-6 series. About 30 were used by 'Sonderkommando Rastedter' in Atlantic service. A further twenty, without the special radio equipment but with tow couplings, were designated He 111 H-14/R2 and served on the Eastern Front. The He 111 H-15 was an H-6 with the ability to carry glide-bombs and remote-controlled weapons.

All the modifications found necessary and incorporated after the H-6 series were brought together in the H-16 main series produced in 1942. The H-16/R1 had an MG 131 machine gun mounted in an electrically-operated dorsal turret. With a towing coupling - in fact a rigid coupling for heavy gliders - it was given the designation H-16/R2, and the R3 was a pathfinder with heavier armour and reduced bomb-carrying capacity.

The He 111 H-18 was a rebuilt H-16 and was used for special duties. The sub-series H-

Left: Many He 111 Hs had their undersides painted black for night action in the West.

Below: Among a group of aircraft photographed at Marienehe, this Heinkel He 111 H-1 still carries its original four-letter code.

18/R3 had the special radio equipment of the H-14. These aircraft were also used as torpedo bombers with the 'Hohentwiel' FuG 200 radar.

The He 111 V46 to V 48 were the prototypes for the H-20 series. They had the H-16 airframe and four different equipment packs which enabled them to be put to various uses, such as troop transports for sixteen paratroopers (R1), transport and tow aircraft (R2), night bombers with heavier armament (R3) and heavy bombers for night service (R4).

At the beginning of 1944 the Jumo 211 gradually began to be replaced by the Jumo 213 of 1,750hp (1,287kW) take-off power. The H-21 series was the first to be given this more powerful engine, but, because of production bottlenecks, the first 22 aircraft were fitted

with the Jumo 211 F with exhaust gas turbocharger. The Jumo 213 did not actually become available until the late autumn of 1944. The H-21 was identical to the H-20/R3, but was structurally strengthened and had a flying weight of 16,000kg. The maximum bomb load, however, only increased to 3,000kg. Without bombs this variant had a maximum speed of 480km/h.

In early 1944 many He 111 H-21s were fitted with launchers for the V 1 (Fi 103), and given the designation H-22, and in the middle of the same year some H-16s and H-20s were also converted to take V-weapons, carrying one Fi 103 on the starboard bomb rack between the hull and the engine nacelle.

The final version of the He 111, produced in the autumn of 1944, was the H-23,

used to drop eight paratroopers with their equipment. This was powered by the Jumo 213 A-1 of 1,780hp (1,308kW) take-off power. However, on reaching their bomber groups, H-23s were re-converted for use as bombers.

A planned high-altitude bomber, the He 111 R, was tried out using one of the H-6 series designated He 111 V 32. This aircraft was tested at the beginning of 1944 using a DB 601 U engine with a TK 9 AC turbocharger. However, it was regarded merely as an interim solution, as the 'Bomber B' programme had not been taken up.

In all, more than 7,300 He 111s were built.

Left: An He 111 H-1 which had clearly taken part in the Spanish Civil War.

Right: A crash landing of an He 111 H-1 of KGr 100 in Northern France.

Right: This He 111 H-1 was attached to KG 55 at Villacoubly in the autumn of 1940, where this ground-crew souvenir photograph was taken.

Opposite page, top: A few Ford V 3000 S tractors were used to pull tanker-trailers by Luftwaffe squadrons stationed in France.

Opposite page, bottom: This 'three-masted' He 111 H-2 of KGr 100 Pathfinder Unit flew over England.

Above: Swinging the compass of an He 111 H-3 of KG 27.

Below: This He 111 H-3 (1H+Ek) was attached to 2/KG 26 and was operated as a pathfinder aircraft.

Left: Some He 111 H-3s were also attached to Flight Leader and Blind Flying Schools. The stripes show that this aircraft, an H-10, was a trainer.

Right: Stationed at Bordeaux, this He 111 H-4 of KG 100 had taken part in several actions over the sea.

Left: An He 111 H-4 of KG 26 in front of a well camouflaged hangar.

Right: Two He 111 H-6s over central Germany.

Opposite page, top: An He 111 H-6 carrying two LT F5b aerial torpedoes.

Left: The He 111 H-6s of KG 27 were stationed in the central sector of the Eastern Front. An Opel 'Blitz' tanker with a standard driver's cab is seen in the foreground.

Above: Refuelling an He 111 H-11 on the Eastern Front, using a captured Russian tanker.

Above: This He 111 H-12 was used for a while in guided-missile tests at the Karlshagen Test Establishment east of Peenemünde.

Below: The He 111 H was also used as a courier aircraft. The machine shown here, together with D-ARQE, D-ALLZ and D-ACLX, was attached to Kontrollinspektion Afrika.

Opposite page, top: An almost complete He 111 H-16 at Marienehe or Oranienburg.

Opposite page, bottom: Two He 111 H-16s of 2./KG 26 during action in Russia at the beginning of 1942.

Left: Loading an SC 1000 bomb, plus graffiti, on to an He 111 H-16.

Right: As a protection against barrage balloon cables, several H-18s were fitted with Kuto-Nase cable-cutting equipment.

Right: The window-mounted MG 81Z beam machine guns represented a considerable improvement in defensive armament in the He 111 H-20.

Left: This He 111 H-18 was flown by Unteroffizier Götz as a pathfinder for KG 100.

Right: The He 111 H-20, seen here over northern Italy near the end of the war, was only produced in small numbers.

Above: The He 111 Z-1 was intended for glider towing. The bomber version, designated Z-2, was never built.

Below: For long-range flights the He 111 Z-1 was equipped with four 900lit drop-tanks. The maximum bomb load was designed to be four SC 1800s.

Dornier Do 217 A, C and E

Below: A wind-tunnel model of a Do 217 E-2 with dive-brakes. In the background is a model of a Do 26.

At the beginning of 1938, manufacturing specification No.1323 for a twin-engined bomber or long-range reconnaissance or smoke-laying aircraft with Daimler-Benz DB 601 B engines was raised, and in February of the same year the RLM gave authority for testing.

Dornier worked on a version of the Do 17 M with the all-round-vision cockpit of the Do 17 Z and a fuselage having a large bomb bay capable of holding a maximum of two 500kg and ten 50kg bombs. For long-range reconnaissance an Rb 50/30 movie camera was fitted

Left: The Kommando Rowehl (Reconnaissance Group of the ObdL) used Do 217 A-0s, but with poor results.

Left: This Do 217 A-0 flew for a short while with II./KG 2 at Soesterberg.

ahead of the front spar of the wing, and an Rb 20/30 was mounted in the second bomb bay. Jettisonable fuel tanks were carried in the forward bomb bay. For smoke-laying, the aircraft could be fitted with two Type S200 smoke generators. Dornier also envisaged the Do 217 as a naval dive-bomber, in which case it was to be fitted with twin floats. In April and May the Do 217 WV1 and WV2 prototypes were produced.

At the end of August 1938 arguments against the floatplane version and in favour of a land-based version to serve as an 'Atlantic Bomber', with its more numerous potential applications, were accepted. At the beginning of January 1939 the RLM stopped all work on the marine dive-bomber, as its estimated performance was inadequate.

On 8 July 1939, therefore, Dornier issued a manufacturing specification for a 'Do 217 E Glide-Bomber for Full Marine Use with BMW 801 Engines'. In contrast to the earlier description, the Do 217 E had a new nose and the nose, cockpit rear, and ventral positions carried one MG 15 each. The maximum bomb load was two SC 500 and two SC 250 bombs, and it was also possible to carry an aerial mine or a torpedo in the bomb bay. A dive brake was fitted to the tail. Flying weight was increased to 10,500kg and the maximum speed was intended to be 530km/h.

The Do 217 V 1 first flew on 4 October 1938, but it crashed seven days later during single-engine flying tests. The second prototype was cleared for flying on 5 November.

Right: The empty bomb bay of a Do 217 C-0.

The third prototype, which was fitted with two Jumo 211 A engines in place of the in-line DB 601s, flew for the first time on 25 February 1939. The same power units were used on the Do 217 V 4 (D-AMSD) which flew in April 1939 at Friedrichshafen and later at Rechlin. These engines were now regarded as essential if the desired performance was to be achieved, and for this reason the fifth test aircraft was fitted with them in June 1939. Later, however, it was given two DB 601 engines, and became the third of six aircraft designated Do 217 A-0 and used for reconnaissance.

The Do 217 V 6 (A-0) was powered by Jumo 211 B engines, but the seventh prototype had BMW 139s and the V 8 (D-AHJE) had BMW 801s. Because the Do 217 A and C were built in only small numbers, and the D and F types remained as projects only, the Do 217 V1E served as the prototype for the Do 217 E-0 series and eventually for the main series. The first flight of the Do 217 E-1 took

Left: The Do 217 V 4 (CN+HL) was identical to the C-0 zero-series aircraft. It was used as a flight-test machine at the Dornier Works in Löwental near Friedrichshafen.

Below left: Two Do 217 D-2s during flight operations over southern Swabia.

Right: Test loading of a Do 217 C-0 with SC 50 bombs.

Below: KG 2 loading a Do 217 E-2 with an LMB (1,000kg).

place on 1 October 1940 at Friedrichshafen. All Do 217 E-series aircraft had two BMW 801 radial engines of 1559hp (1,147kW) take-off power. In addition to three MG 15s, there was also a fixed 20mm gun built into the nose. The majority of the aircraft were capable of carrying sixteen SC 50 bombs or one SC 1800. Alternatively, they could carry two LMA aerial mines or one LT F 5 torpedo. The E-2 version could carry one additional LMB aerial mine.

The prototype of the Do 217 E-2 series, V 18, differed from the E-1 notably in its heavier armament, having a DL 131/1 rotary mounting in the cockpit rear position and one MG 131 in the ventral position, as well as the cable cutting nose. In addition, the maximum bomb load was increased to 4,000kg. The Do 217 E-1 and E-2

with full military equipment and two 900lit drop tanks under the outer wings had a range of 3,700km, and maximum speed was around 485km/h. The majority of these aircraft went to KG 2 and KG 40, where they replaced the Do 17.

The Do 217 E-4 was identical to the E-2 apart from the heavy MG-FF in the nose. This version was intended especially for marine service. For use with glider bombs, the E-4 had an additional wing-mounted ETC 2000/XII and the FuG 203 B 'Kehl III' radio-control system, and was given the designation E-5. It first saw action on 25 August 1943 against Allied naval forces in the Bay of Biscay.

The Do 217 E-6 was a dual-control conversion, and came into use in 1943 in several training establishments.

Below: This Do 217 E-2 flew as a pathfinder for I./KG 66 from airfields in the Netherlands and Northern France.

Right: This Do 217, which served as pathfinder for I./KG 66, flew without fixed 20mm armament. Often, the side window mounts were also removed.

Bottom right: This Do 217 E-4 (Works No.4305) was attached to III./KG 2. After several had been lost in night actions, the BMW 801 MA engine exhausts were fitted with flare guards.

Above: A Do 217 E-4 (9./KG 5, U5+ET) taking off at Soesterberg. Its targets were mainly harbours and industry in southern England.

Left: Changing the engine of a Do 217 E-2 of KG 2 at Colounmiers.

Right: Loading a Do 217 E-2 of III./KG 2 with SC 500 bombs in the winter of 1942/43.

Below: Recovery of a Do 217 E-4 (4./KG 40, F8+KM) in France at the end of 1942.

Left: A collision at Amsterdam-Schiphol airport on 12 August 1942, in which a Do 217 E-4 (Works No.4263, U5+DT) was badly damaged.

Right: A well-camouflaged pathfinder aircraft of II./KG 6 runs up at Montdidier.

Left: Recovery operations on a Do 217 E-4 after the undercarriage collapsed on landing, damaging the propeller and airframe.

Left: Servicing a Do 217 of I./KG 66.

Right: Because of the danger of attacks from deep-penetration raiders, aircraft were parked well apart. This is a Do 217 E-4 of III./KG 100 at Istres.

Above: The Do 217 E-5s of KG 100 served mainly for carrying guided missiles using 900lit drop-tanks.

Below: Many retired Do 217 E-2, E-4, and E-5 aircraft were converted to dual-control trainers, classified E-6, and used at Flight Leader and Blind Flying schools.

Dornier Do 217 K and M

At the beginning of 1942, tests on a new, larger canopy for the Do 217 began in a towing tank at the Hamburger Schiffbauanstalt (Hamburg Shipbuilding Institute). Aircraft from the E-2 series were fitted with this canopy, and initial flight testing took place on 31 March 1942, after some structural difficulties had been resolved. The first of two BMW 801 A-1 powered Do 217 KV 1s flew first of all from Löwenthal and later from Rechlin. It was followed by the zero-series models Do 217 K-01 to K-10.

Mass production of the Do 217 K-1 began at the Dornier factory at Wismar in North Germany, using the 1,559hp (1,147kW) BMW 801 engine. Armament consisted of one MG 81Z in the nose and one MG 131 at the dorsal and ventral positions. Two to four MG 81 guns could also be mounted in the cabin side windows. With an average flying weight of 12,700kg, this aircraft achieved a speed of 520km/h at 5,200m. A few K-1s were converted as Do 217 E-4s.

The equipment of the K-2 series was the same as that of the K-1, but the wing area was increased by 67m². These aircraft were used for glider-bombing, carrying two PC 1400 X missiles. In the summer of 1943 three aircraft were fitted with launchers for the Hs 293 radio-controlled glider-bomb, and were then designated Do 217 K-2/U1. Most had the same equipment as the K-1, but some machines had a rigid tail-

Below: A Do 217 K-1 of 8./KG 2 in the summer of 1943, during retraining for conversion of E-4s to K-1s.

mounted MG 81Z, which, however, did not prove especially useful.

The last of the K-series was the K-3, another guided-missile carrier (Fritz X, Hs 293), which was converted from the Do 217 M-1 in the late summer of 1943 and given the larger wing of the K-2. When fitted with the fuselage-mounted ETC external weapons carrier this aircraft was designated K-3/U1, and had improved defensive armament in the form of one MG 81 Z and one MG 81 I in the nose. The Do 217 K-3 was built in only very limited numbers.

Because of the increasing requirement for BMW 801 radial engines to be used in Focke-Wulf Fw 190 production, the Do 217 M was fitted with DB 603 A-1 in-line engines from May 1942. As a result of problems with this engine, which was still not fully developed, the first flight of the Do 217 MV 1 did not take place until 16 July 1942. After this, the aircraft went into mass production until the summer of the following year. The zero series (M-01 to M-03) had Works Nos.1241 to 1243. Apart from the engine, the M-1 basically corresponded to the K-1. The defensive armament of the level-bomber and dive-bomber versions consisted of one MG 131 in the nose, two MG 81 I in the cabin side windows, and two MG 131 in the dorsal and ventral positions. The two M-1/U2 aircraft (Works Nos.1244 and 1245) had 'Kehl IV' radio control apparatus and could carry either two PC1400X or two Hs 293 glider bombs. The Do 217 M-1/U5 was the prototype for the installation of the TK-9 turbocharger.

The aerial torpedo version, Do 217 M-2, had the airframe of the M-1 with normal wings plus the necessary torpedo-carrying equipment, giving a maximum flying weight of 16,700kg. The prototype, bearing the code letters GB+CY, was test-flown in May 1942, and torpedo drop tests followed on June 17-20. On 21 June 1943, however, this aircraft was destroyed during tests on a new type of torpedo at Gotenhafen. This version never went into mass production, because the RLM chose the Ju 88 as its standard torpedo bomber.

In December 1943 Dornier issued the specification for the Do 217 M-3. It was to be a heavy bomber with a four-man crew, a wing area of 59m², a wingspan of 19.8m, and the first mass-produced tricycle undercarriage. Power for this 16,700kg machine would be provided by two DB 603 engines. The prototype was a Do 217 M-1 with the wings from a K-2. In November, however, it was cancelled by the Technische Amt (Technical Department of the RLM) in favour of the more powerful Ju 188, as was the specially-armed, turbocharged M-4 design. The prototype (GB+CV) flew several times between 16 Dec 1942 and 23 Feb 1944 at Rechlin.

The missile-carrying M-5 was another version that did not go into mass production.

The Do 217 M-8 represented the end of exhaust-gas turbocharging development at

Above: Aircraft U5+CS (8./KG 2) was used as a trainer for a time.

Opposite page, top: A Do 217 K-1 of II./KG 2 attached to units at Glize-Rijn in the autumn of 1943.

Opposite page, bottom: The Do 217 K-2 was a development of the Do 217 K-1 with increased wingspan. The aircraft shown (KG 100) was damaged on landing at Kalamaki on 15 November 1943.

Above: The Do 217 K-07 (Works No.4407, RD+JF) was used from January 1943 as a torpedo bomber, carrying up to four LTF 5s.

Left: The Do 217 HV 3 served, together with two other Do 217 Hs, as a flying test bed for the DB 603 A in-line engine.

Right: This Do 217 K-1, U5+DR, seen here during a brief coffee break in the spring of 1943, was attached to 7./KG 2.

Below: Warning of night-fighter attack from the rear was given by an FuG 216 Neptun R radar in this Do 217 M-1 (Works No.722753) of 7./KG 2 (note antennae under the wings).

Dornier. The prototype (PQ+WP) flew at Rechlin in May 1943. With its wing area increased to 67m², this 17,200kg heavy bomber was intended for high-altitude applications, but was cancelled by the RLM. The two prototypes and both test models had to be cannibalised for parts. The M-9 (KE+JN, Works No. 0040), a conversion of the Do 217 K-1, resembled the M-3 but had the greater wing area (67m²), and could carry two PC 1400X or one to two Hs 293 missiles. Its armament consisted of two MG 131, one MG 151, and two MG 81 machine guns.

The M-10 was a planned conversion of the M-1, with wings made from reclaimed materials to save valuable wood and steel, but, after some development work at Wismar, it too was cancelled by the RLM. The M-11 did go into mass production; it was a special operations aircraft with one PC 1400 X missile slung

under the fuselage. The majority went to KG 100 from May 1944. They were powered by the DB 603 A-2, with four-bladed propellers and exhaust flare shields. Their defensive armament consisted of three MG 131s and two MG 81s, as well as — in some isolated cases — the tail-mounted armament of the K-2 and K-3 series.

At the end of 1941 Dornier investigated the possibilities of a heavy dive-bomber, the Do 217 R, based on the E-1 but with the K-1 cockpit and greater wingspan. Work was stopped at the end of 1943, and both test aircraft, RV1 (TC+ZC, Works No.0029) and RV2 (DB+BA, Works No.0030) were scrapped. The RV 3 and 4 were never built.

Below: A Do 217 M-1 group during transfer. The central aircraft (U5+CX) was attached to 13./KG 2.

Bottom: This Do 217 M-11 was lost over northern France while returning from a bombing mission in the summer of 1944.

Junkers Ju 88 A

In August 1935 the RLM drew up the tactical requirements for an unarmed, three-seat, high-speed bomber with a military payload of 800kg to 1,000kg. In November 1935 Henschel, Messerschmitt and Junkers received invitations to tender for this aircraft. Junkers presented the RLM with their first model of the future Ju 88 in June 1936. As a result, they were given the go-ahead to build two 'High-Speed Bombers' (Works Nos.4941 and 4942) of 2,000km range, powered by two DB 600 engines, and also a further three aircraft (Works Nos.4943 to 4945), powered by Junkers Jumo 211 engines, as a pre-series batch.

The Ju 88 V1 and V2 were unarmed high-speed bombers with three-man crews. In contrast, V3 to V5 had three defensive armament positions, improved equipment, and the ability to carry two 1,000kg bombs under the inboard wing panels. The next stage was a complete redesign to produce a heavy dive-bomber with greater range, a four-man crew, stronger wings, a larger undercarriage, and an extended fuselage.

Right: A wind tunnel model of the Ju 85, a twin-finned bomber which never went into production.

Left: The mock-up of the cockpit and ventral turret of the Ju 85 at Dessau.

Bottom left: The Ju 88 V 2 (Works No.4912, D-ASAZ) during inspection by representatives of the Technische Amt of the RLM at the Rechlin Research Establishment.

Below: After replacement of its DB 600 Cs by Jumo 211 in-line engines, the Ju 88 V 2 was assigned as a trainer in the Nuremburg region and designated VA+EG.

On 21 December 1936, about a year later, the Ju 88 V1 made its first flight, but only part of the test programme had been carried out when the aircraft crashed on 10 April 1937. On the same day, the V2 flew for the first time. The radiator area of this aircraft was found to be too small, requiring structural modifications. Eventually it was given a new nose section and later served in various roles during the development of the Ju 288.

The Ju 88 V 3 (D-AREN, Works No.4943) first flew on 13 September 1937. It was powered by Jumo 211 A engines and reached a maximum speed of 520km/h during tests at Rechlin. The RLM therefore requested rapid further development of the Jumo 211 engine in readiness for mass production, because the majority of Daimler-Benz engines were destined for fighters.

In October 1937 Generalluftzeugmeister Ernst Udet ordered the development of the Ju 88 as a heavy dive-bomber, rather than the unarmed high-speed bomber originally proposed. This decision was supported by the unexpected success of the Ju 87 in its dive-bomber role. In December the RLM ordered intensive further development of the Ju 88, and

the Junkers development division at Dessau was therefore reinforced. Special emphasis was given to the study of dive brakes and automatic pull-out systems.

On 24 February 1938 the Ju 88 V 3 crashed near Nüremberg while on a secret record flight over a range of 2,000km carrying a 2,000kg bomb load. Some two weeks earlier, on 2 February, the V 4 model (D-ASYT) had made its first flight. Along with the V 6 model (D-AQKD), it was intended as the test aircraft for the required heavy dive-bomber version, and so became the prototype for the planned A-1 series of the Ju 88.

The Ju 88 V 5 (D-ATYU, Works No.4945), took to the air for the first time on 13 April 1938. It had an extended cockpit and the more powerful Jumo 211 B-1 in-line engines, and was used, still unarmed, for high-speed testing. Numerous tests on dive brakes were also carried out on this aircraft.

The previously mentioned V 6 (D-AQKD) made its maiden flight on 28 June 1938. As the first prototype of the Ju 88, it was fitted with what was called 'central control'. As with the V 5, this aircraft had four-bladed propellers, and, like the A-1 series, a second bomb bay.

Left: Among the first groups to be equipped with Ju 88 A-1s was I./KG 30; these aircraft had several problems initially.

Below left: This Ju 88 A-1 was used for factory tests. Note the partial armouring on the ventral position.

Below: A brand new Ju 88 A-1 has its compass swung at the factory.

The V 6 was the first Ju 88 to use dive brakes under realistic conditions.

In the autumn of 1938 Heinrich Koppenberg stated that production of 300 Ju 88s per month was definitely possible. Reichsmarschall Göring was in favour of the production of the Ju 88 A-1, and gave absolute priority to the provision of the necessary materials. For this purpose, the Volkswagenwerk at Wolfsburg and the Opel-Werk at Rüsselsheim were enlisted as suppliers. Final assembly took place simultaneously at the JFM-Werke at Aschersleben, Halberstadt, Leopoldshall, and Bernburg. The first test machine for the series was the V 7 (D-ARNC). This dive-bomber had two Jumo 211 engines driving VS 11 variable-pitch propellers. It flew for the first time on 27 September 1938. A year later it was converted into a high-speed transport, with the bomb bay area now containing a four-seat passenger cabin.

When many bombers became victims of British balloon barrages, the Ju 88 V 7 was equipped with a cable-cutter and was successfully tested in this role. It was then used for test flights with the nose section of the Ju 88 A-1 fitted. Later still came dive tests with SC 250 and SC 500 bombs, and, from January 1940, with the heavier SC 1000 and SD 1000 bombs.

The first flight of the Ju 88 V 8 (DG+BF, Works No.4948) took place on 3 October 1938, and the zero-series began with the V 9 and V 10 models, followed by three A-1 models with Works Nos.0003 to 0005. Some of the A-1 series aircraft were fitted with the Kuto-Nase balloon-cable cutting equipment at the

Rechlin Test Establishment, and also had enlarged dive brakes and more streamlined external bomb racks.

The Ju 88 A-1s were powered by Jumo 211 B-1 or G engines and had variable-pitch propellers. Their defensive armament consisted of one MG 15 in the nose, and first one and later two MG 15 in the rear cockpit, with a further MG 15 in a ventral gondola. They could carry two SC 1000 bombs under the inboard wing panels, or an equivalent load of SC 50 or SC 250 bombs in the bomb bay. The maximum weight of the A-1 series increased to 12,300kg owing to essential modifications. Use of the similarly-powered but more robust Jumo 211 G-1 and the fitting of catapult mounts for high-load take-offs led to the A-2, under which designation the main series was intended to

run. After only a few models (converted A-1s) had been built, however, production was abandoned when the requirement for catapult launching was dropped.   At the same time, a few A-1 airframes were converted for dual control and served as trainers, designated Ju 88 A-3.

The first test model of the A-4 series, the Ju 88 V 21 (D-ACBO), flew on 1 November 1940. After tests as a bomber it became the D-1 prototype (armed reconnaissance aircraft), and six months of development work followed, in which the more powerful Jumo 211 J engine played an important part and the wing area was

Left: This Ju 88 A-1 (9K+HS) was attached to 8./KG 51 'Edelweiss'; it is seen soon after arrival, still unarmed.

Below left: This Ju 88 A-1 (4D+AH) was attached to 1.Squadron of KG 30, and in the summer of 1941 flew from Norway on missions against Allied shipping.

Below: This Ju 88 A-1 airframe (L1+HK) was fitted with the wings of an A-5. It was attached to 2./Training Group 1.

increased. Defensive armament was also beefed up by the fitting of MG 81 I and Z machine guns. For ship- or ground-attack missions, a 20mm FF cannon could be fitted in the nose at any time.

The Ju 88 A-5 had the extended wings and could carry a maximum external load of one SC 1800 and one SC 1000 on the inboard wing racks. Fuel capacity was now 3,580lit.

By August 1940 the heavy dive-bombers (Ju 88 A-1 and A-5) were reaching operational units in greater numbers, with the dive-bomber version of the A-4 following somewhat later. Furthermore, in the autumn of 1940 Junkers also delivered increased numbers of Ju 88 A-5 aircraft with one of five MG 15s or one 20mm MG FF in the nose, and MG 81 Zs in defensive positions.

This was followed by the fitting of five MG 81s in place of the older MG 15s. When the newer A-4 and A-5 aircraft became available, the older versions were sent to flying schools for use as trainers.

A few Ju 88 A-5s were temporarily fitted with balloon-cable cutters and powered by two Jumo B/G engines, then being given the designation A-6. Some A-5s were converted for dual control and used as auxiliary trainers (Ju 88 A-7). After the use of the A-6 as a cable-cutter,

Left: Dipl-Ing Zindel gives expert advice on an early Ju 88 A-5.

Right: An early Ju 88 A-5, not yet fitted with bomb racks, attached to a group in the west.

Right: A Ju 88 D-1 in southern Italy in 1942, used for armed reconnaissance.

the A-8 version was fitted with the new 'Kuto-nase' equipment, which proved easier to use than the cutting gear on the A-6.

Three tropicalised versions followed: the A-9, a converted A-1, the A-10, converted from the A-5, and the A-11, which was given the Jumo 211 engine, extensive tropical equipment, and in fact corresponded to the unit machines of the A-4 series.

From 1943 some A-5s were given a wider fuselage and used as trainers, type A-12. The A-4s which were converted for training were designated A-16.

The low-level-attack version A-13 existed only in the form of trials aircraft with modified bomb racks. It was found to be impossible to incorporate different weapons mounts (WB 151/20) without extensive reconstruction.

In the late summer of 1942 the first two A-14 test aircraft flew at Dessau. This type was a development of the A-4, and was fitted with the Kuto-Nase. It could carry two ETC 1000 bombs under the inboard wings and had the nose-mounted MG FF as standard. Some were given different nose armament. Conversion of the Ju 88 A-4 with newer bomb dropping equipment and other modifications produced the A-15 'special bomber'. The RLM did not authorise mass production, however, as the speed was reduced too much by the bulged wooden bomb bay.

Finally, there was the A-17 torpedo carrier. The airframe was that of the A-4, but there was no ventral gun position.

Left: This Ju 88 A-5 was attached to 1./KG 77 of Luftflotte 2 in Italy, in the summer of 1943.

Below left: A Ju 88 A-5 (Works No.2087) attached to a Flight Leader School C.

Above: A Ju 88 A-5 (L1+IM) of 4./LG 1 in flight over the Mediterranean.

Below: Apparently a difference of opinion between the Company Sergeant and a member of Ground Crew. The aircraft, a Ju 88 A-5 (3Z+BH) was in action in the central sector of the Eastern Front.

Above: Maintenance work on a Jumo 211 in-line engine of a Ju 88 A-5 of KG 54. Note the extended dive-brakes.

Left: A Ju 88 A-5 brought down by Russian flak in the southern sector of the Eastern Front. Clearly visible is the radio equipment, as well as the windshield-mounted MG 15.

Top right: This Ju 88 A-5 (4D+EM) attached to II./KG 30 has a 20mm MG FF cannon in the nose and is thus equipped for deep-penetration attacks.

Right: A Ju 88 A-6 converted for training. The earlier mounts for balloon cable cutting equipment are still clearly visible.

Left: The solemn funeral of the Born Crew (Junkers Works) in Dessau. The aircraft in the background are Ju 88 A-4s.

Right: Hauptmann Helbig (LG 1) was the pilot of this Ju 88 A-4, which had an MG FF cannon mounted above the bomb sight.

Left: This Ju 88 A-4 (Works No.6672) was part of III./KG 3. An MG 81Z is mounted in the rear of the ventral gondola.

Right: A Ju 88 A-4 of II./KG 30 ready for loading an AB 1000 drop canister at Griffon in 1944.

Left: A Ju 88 A-4 attached to II./KG 3 'Blitz' is cleared of snow.

Below left: The 'Steinbock' attacks on England in early 1944 involved this Ju 88 A-4, equipped with flare guards and an AB 1000 canister which held 610 B-1 incendiary bombs.

Above: The transfer to Italy of a Ju 88 A-4 (B3+AT) of III./KG 54.

Right: This Ju 88 A-4 (Works No.550396, B3+MH) of 1./KG 54 landed at Dübendorf, Switzerland, on 21 October 1943 after the crew had lost their bearings.

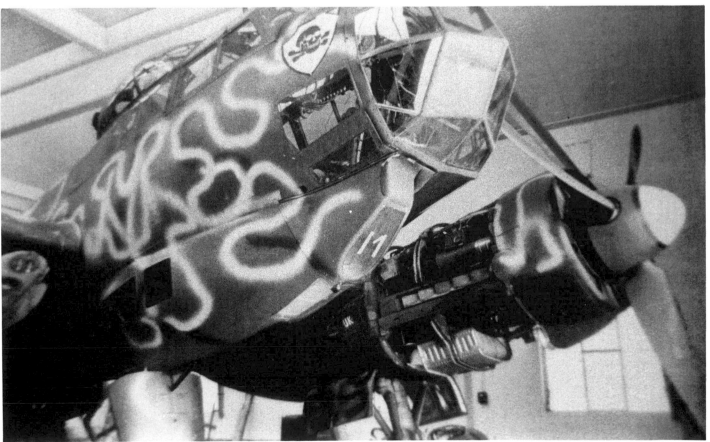

Left: A KG 77 crew pose with their camouflaged Ju 88 A-4.

Below left: A bomber unit carries on despite adverse conditions on the central sector of the Eastern Front in the autumn of 1943.

Above: One of the remaining Ju 88 A-4s or A-14s of I./KG 54, before it was re-equipped with Me 262s.

Right: The main difference between the A-4 and the A-14 was the fitting of an MG FF cannon in the nose as standard.

Junkers Ju 88 B

Left: The prototype of the Ju 88 A-15 had no influence on the later series. Only in the Ju 388 were similar bomb bays fitted.

Below left: A full-scale mock-up of the Ju 85 B, which led directly to the Ju 88 B with improved cabin glazing and, eventually, to the Ju 188.

Below: The defensive armament of the Ju 85 B was at first intended to be three MG 15s.

As early as 1936 Junkers had a variant of the Ju 85 with an all-round-vision cockpit similar to that of the Do 217. The RLM, however, preferred the conventional cockpit and ordered production of the Ju 88 A-1. Nevertheless, Junkers continued to work on versions of the Ju 88 B-1 to B-4 fitted with the full-vision canopy (the 'Kampfkopf', or 'Combat Head'), and received an order to build prototype Ju 88s BV 23 to BV 32. Construction began in July 1939 and many parts of the Ju 88 A-5 were used. At the end of 1940 the test aircraft were fitted with Jumo 211 B/F or BMW 801 two-row radial engines. The test flight programme demonstrated the considerably better performance of the Ju 88 B, which could reach 530km/h with a 2,000kg bomb load. At least two of the Ju 88 B test models (BV 27 and 30) were fitted with an MG 131 rotary turret in the 'Kampfkopf'. This version was given the designation Ju 88 E-0 and was the forerunner of the Ju 188 E-1.

The planned Ju 88 E-1 series was intended to have the 151/20 rotary turret and to be pow-

ered by the Jumo 213 B engine, but it never went into mass production, being cancelled in favour of the Ju 188. However, 23 Ju 88 E-1 aircraft were ordered by the RLM in March 1942 and, from this version, Junkers developed the Ju 88 reconnaissance aircraft with equipment from the Ju 88 D. This project also failed because of the requirement for mass production of the Ju 188 E and F.

The Ju 88 C was used almost exclusively as a night-fighter and 'Zerstörer' (heavy fighter), and the same applied to the long-range-reconnaissance Ju 88 D and the Ju 88 G-1 to G-10 night-fighters. Some Ju 88 Hs with extended fuselages may have been used for long-range reconnaissance over the Bay of Biscay.

The Ju 88 S high-speed bomber developed from the Ju 88 A will be covered in Chapter IV. The last Ju 88 bombers of the A-4 series, attached to KG 6, 30, and 54, were lost over England.

Left: The Ju 88 BV23 flew for the first time on 19 June 1940.

Below: In February 1942 the airframe of the Ju 88 BV26 was sent from the Versuchsstelle für Höhenflüge (VfH - High-Altitude Research Establishment) at Oranienburg to Dessau, for repair following a particularly hard landing.

Above: The Ju 88 BV27 shows all the armament of the Ju 188 A and E. In addition to an MG 151/20 in the nose, MG 131s were provided in both front and rear dorsal positions.

Right: A conversion of the Ju 88 BV27 for research purposes led eventually to the Ju 88 E and E-1 series.

Above: Use of an MG 151 Z mount was also modelled, as here on a Ju 88 B.

Left: The aft dorsal position of this Ju 188 E-1 is equipped with an MG 151, and the lower position with an MG 131.

Junkers Ju 188

The transformation of the Ju 88 into the Ju 188 was similar to that of the Do 217 E into its K and M versions. The Ju 88 V 4 was introduced in mid-1942 and resembled the V 27 aircraft apart from having the larger tail unit of the Ju 88 G-1. In October 1942, however, it became apparent that neither the Jumo 222 engine nor the Ju 288 aircraft were yet ready for mass production, so the Ju 88 V 44 became the prototype for the Ju 188 design. It was later redesignated Ju 188 V 1, and a sec-

ond test aircraft was prepared. Both machines were sent for testing by EK 188 in January 1943, and trials of stability and flight characteristics took place the following June. Armament testing, especially of the tail guns, took place at Tarnewitz.

During preparation for mass production of the Ju 188 at Bernburg, the RLM issued a requirement that the aircraft should be able to accept either the Jumo 213 in-line or the BMW 801 radial without alterations to the engine

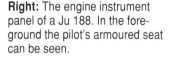

Right: The engine instrument panel of a Ju 188. In the foreground the pilot's armoured seat can be seen.

Left: Side view of an MG 131 I, which was intended to be used, for example, in the Ju 188 E-1 or the planned G-2.

Left: The heavy armament in the nose of the Ju 188 A and E series was an MG 151/20. This gun was also intended for the Ju 188 G series.

Right: The Ju 188 V 1 was tested at Rechlin between September and November 1943 with a manually controlled tail gun position fitted with an HL 131 Z/1 mounting and VE 47 sights.

Below: This Ju 188 E-1 was used for factory testing at Junkers in Dessau.

Above: A Ju 188 A-2 of I./KG 6. These aircraft served mainly as pathfinders with this unit.

Left: These Ju 188 E-1s were captured intact at the end of the war

housing. From this requirement came the Ju 188 A- and E-series with the Jumo and BMW engines respectively, the E-1 going into production first and being delivered in the second quarter of 1943. Both series had one MG 151/20 in the nose, one in the cabin roof with a rotary mount for MG 131 (Ju 188 E) or MG 151 (Ju 188 A), to the rear of that a second dorsal position with one MG 131, and a ventral position with an MG 81 Z. The maximum bomb load was 3,000kg, giving an all-up weight of 14,500kg. Some 500 Ju 188s of the A and E series were manufactured up to the summer of 1944, when production ceased, and they were very positively received by the aircrew who flew them.

The first Ju 188 powered by the 1,776hp (1,306kW) Jumo 213 A-1 engine was assem-

bled at Bernburg in the early summer of 1943. It was now intended for level bombing, carrying up to sixteen SD 65s in the bomb bay and a drop load of up to 2,000kg on four underwing racks. Its wingspan was 22.0m, and maximum speed was about 510km/h.

Like the E-series, the Ju 188 A-1 had originally been designed as a dive-bomber, but production was discontinued in favour of the A-2, which from the beginning of 1944 was solely intended for level-flight bombing. The Jumo 213 A-1 engine was given a methanol-water injection system (MW 50), which increased take-off power to 2,241hp (1,648kW).

Because of the inadequate rear defence against attacking fighter aircraft, a test aircraft was equipped with a manually-controlled tail gun position. The armament of this Ju 188 C-0 was intended to be two MG 131s mounted one above the other. The Ju 188 V 2 also had a tail gun position and in this form corresponded to the projected Ju 188 G.

In the torpedo-bomber version, the Ju 188 A-3, two of the four external bomb racks were removed so that the aircraft could carry either two LT 1B or two LT F5b aerial torpedoes. A blister on the starboard side of the nose contained the guidance system for the aerial torpedoes (LT), and the antennae for the FuG 200 marine search radar were also fitted in the nose area.

The Ju 188 E, powered by the BMW 801 ML engine, was another dive-bomber version. It began its flight-testing in the first part of 1943. Apart from the MG 131 in the foremost dorsal position, armament was the same as that of the Ju 188 A, as were overall dimensions, bomb load, and power. The E-1 did, however, have additional dive brakes and automatic pull-out equipment. Also with the E-1 came the more powerful 1,700hp (1,250kW) BMW 801 D-2 and G-2 engines. Later, when the dive-bomber concept had been dropped, the last E-1 came off the production line as a conventional bomber. The torpedo-bomber version, the Ju 188 E-2, was identical to the A-3 apart from the powerplant.

The Ju188 served with Kampfgesch-waders 2, 6, 26, and 65, as well as with 1.(F)/120 and 3.(F)/122 squadrons.

The planned MG 131 Z tail-gun position in the Ju 188 G was abandoned as unfeasible. The traverse of the gun was limited, so that only very light arms could be mounted in the rear turret, with the gunner in a crouching position. The remote-controlled FA 15 tail mounting was still at an early stage of development and was not yet available. The Luftwaffe rejected the manned position and approved the further development of the remote-controlled FA 15 mounts for both MG 131s, intending them to go into production with the G-2 version. However, because of the run-up to the Ju 388, this version never entered production.

The planned Ju 188 K series was designed with a pressurised cabin, and became the high-altitude K and L versions of the Ju 388.

Only a few test aircraft of the high-speed, high-altitude Ju 188 S-1 with the Jumo 213 E-1 engine and pressurised cabin were produced. The S-1 airframe was later used by Junkers for the pre-series of the Ju 388 L-0 high-altitude reconnaissance aircraft.

The last Ju 188 captured by the British was an A-3 (1H+AT, Works No.190335) of 9./KG 26 squadron, which landed at Fraserburgh on 2 May 1945 and surrendered without resistance.

Below: At least one Ju 188 A-2 was used by the RAF for flights between Denmark and England in the summer of 1945.

Heinkel He 177

The designations 'Bomber A' and 'Bomber B' were the respective development definitions for a long-range and a more powerful mid-range bomber. On 6 August 1937 the initial viewing of a test model of the Heinkel He P 1041 took place at Rostock Marienehe, but, because of inadequate crew space and poor instrumentation, many modifications proved necessary. A second viewing then took place on 11 November 1937. An unusual feature of this aircraft was the use of two pairs of Daimler-Benz DB 601 A/E engines (i.e., DB 601 A engines brought up to E standard), each pair being coupled to make a DB 606 engine unit and driving a single propeller. Additionally, a long-range bomber variant with four single engines in separate nacelles was being developed.

The twin-engined version of the P 1041 was a dive-bomber suitable for long-range ser-

vice, and the project was officially given the designation He 177 on 5 November 1937. After several model viewings, Heinkel began unit and component production in 1939.

The He 177 V 1 (CB+RP, Works No.00001) took off for the first time on 20 November 1939 with Lt Francke at the controls. In April 1940 the V 2 (CBN+RQ) and V 3 (D-AGIG) prototypes followed, and by the beginning of 1941 four further pre-production aircraft had been produced. On 24 April 1940 the V 3 was lost at Geldorf, and the V 2 (Graal/Müritz) was crashed on 27 June 1940. On 8 June 1941 the V 4 model was also lost owing to an engine fire.

Up to the autumn of 1941, the Rechlin test programme had been subject to delays due to bad weather and numerous engine problems. The He 177 V 8 (SF+TC) and the second zero-series aircraft (A-02) were therefore given

Below: The He 177 V 2 (Works No.177 000003), which had to be completely written off after a crash on 26 June 1940.

enlarged cowlings, which considerably increased the service life of the DB 606 engine.

The first dive tests took place in March 1942, but on 16 July the A-103 model crashed because of over-severe pull-outs during the Rechlin flight tests. It had been used for trials of the extension flaps, enlarged engine cowlings, and an enlarged rudder, as well as for cold-start and other tests. Further delays to the test programme were caused by problems with supplies of components (e.g. coupling sleeves), but Heinkel's request to transfer the test programme to Marienehe was denied.

During 1940-41, mass production of the He 177 A-0 took place at the Heinkel works at Marienehe and Oranienburg, as well as at the Arado works at Warnemünde. After production of 35 of the zero series, the Arado works at Brandenburg and Warnemünde then produced under licence a further 130 He 177 A-1s, for which the He 177 V 12 was the prototype. The A-1 differed from the A-0 in that it had six additional ETC 2000 XIIIB. It could carry a maximum bomb load of 2,200kg. Defensive armament consisted of one MG 81 in the upper and one MG-FF in the lower nose positions, an MG 81Z installed in the ventral position, and an MG 131 in the remote-controlled dorsal turret. The tail gun was also an MG 131. The A-1/R2 model was used to try out an MG 131 in the rearmost ventral position, behind which lay the spacious bomb bay. The final development of the A-1, the He 177 A-1/R4, had single MG

131s in the rearmost dorsal and the ventral positions. Up to June 1942, twelve He 177 A-1s were converted to He 177 A-1/U2 long-range heavy fighters with two MK 101s in the lower nose. Two or three were transferred to the long-range heavy-fighter squadron of KG 40, then being re-formed (first as 10./KG 40, then 15./KG 40, and finally as 17 squadron), but they were not used against Allied bombers over the Atlantic. American B-17s and B-24s were able to arrive in Britain unmolested.

The thorough evaluation of all previous flight trials led to 170 improvements and 1,395 structural modifications. However, structural problems recurred in September 1942 in the region of the wing, especially in angled flight or dives. Yet, despite everything, Professor Heinkel's request that the requirement for this large aircraft to have diving capability be dropped fell on deaf ears at the Technische Amt. In the end, Göring himself, on 15 September 1942, ordered the He 177 diving requirement to be dropped. From then on the aircraft was only to be used in horizontal flight, as in Operation Steinbock at the beginning of 1944. Engine problems remained, however. In tests, the maximum speed available was 515km/h (440km/h at low level), and, with four SC 250 bombs, penetration range was 2,400km.

From October, a new main series of He 177 A-3 aircraft with the new DB 610 engine, which comprised two DB 605s coupled

Below: On 3 October 1941 the He 177 V 1 (CB+RP) suffered 50 per cent damage during landing.

Above: The He 177 V 4 was also written off: it was lost on June 8, 1941 as a result of an unintentional ground contact.

Left: The He 177 V 8 was extensively tested with shortened Fowler flaps and a modified powerplant

Above: A remote-controlled nose gun position was tested on this He 177 A-1 (Works No.15155) at Rechlin experimental establishment.

together, was built by Arado at Brandenburg and Heinkel at Oranienburg. But the new engine had not been fully tested, and more problems arose with cooling and oil circulation, so that up to January 1943 all aircraft were still delivered with the DB 606. At the same time, endurance testing of the DB 610 began at Lärz near Rechlin, using the first eight He 177s of the A-3 series. In addition, 40 aircraft, some from the A-1 and others from the A-3 series, were fitted with GM-1 fuel injection to increase power. Various difficulties with the tests, such as poor hydraulics, many delays due to accidents, modification work on test aircraft, production bottlenecks, and especially the inadequate production of DB 605 engines led to delays. Yet another problem was that the majority of DB 605 production was reserved for fighter aircraft, so that by the beginning of February 1943 there was a shortfall of 200 engines. More and more He 177s were left without engines, a condition which persisted until the end of the war. In the end, airframes were simply scrapped. Furthermore, the flying weight of the He 177 had crept up to some 34,000kg, requiring a reduction in fuel capacity in order to keep to the design take-off weight. Tactical range was therefore severely

restricted. In addition, defensive armament was adapted to suit future mission conditions.

So, in addition to airframe modifications, the He 177 A-3 had an MG 151/20 as a tail gun instead of the MG 131. In this version, permissible bomb load was also increased to 2,500kg. The He 177 A-3/R3 was equipped with an FuG 203 for use with two to three Hs 293 guided missiles. The defensive armament was the same as that of the A-3/R1 and R2 models, and the powerplant was the DB 610 A/B double engine. The R4 type was given a 'Kehl III' radio-control system, and could therefore carry the PC 1400 X or Hs 293 A-1 missiles. With the advent of the He 177 A-3/R7, the Luftwaffe had a more powerful long-range bomber. However, the additional fuel tanks meant that the rear bomb bay could only be used for dropping free-falling bombs.

The He 177 A-3/R7 was planned as a torpedo bomber which, with partial reduction in defensive armament, would have the capability to carry four LT5 torpedoes, but in the end it served only as a prototype.

Later, a few He 177 A-1s were converted to A-3 form. The planned high-altitude bomber versions, A-2 and A-4, were cancelled because the conversion costs appeared to be too high.

Mass production of the A-5 model, of which eventually at least 565 were to be produced, was begun by Arado and Heinkel in October 1943. This was a direct development of the A-3 with heavier defensive armament and bomb load increased to 2,800kg. The He 177 A-5/R1 also served as a carrier for Hs 293 A-1/B-1 and PC 1400 X glider bombs. Its defensive armament consisted of one MG 81 I in the upper nose position, one MG 151/20 in the lower nose position, one FDL B 131/2A with an MG 131 in the foremost dorsal position, one MG 131 in the rearmost dorsal position, one MG 81 Z in the ventral position and one MG 151/20 as a tail gun. The R2 type was identical apart from an MG 131 replacing the MG 81 Z in the ventral position, and the division of the bomb bay into three sections. Further strengthening of the defensive armament took place in the A-5/R3 type. In addition to the armament of the R2, an MG 131 was installed in the ventral position. With the He 177 A-5/R5 an FDL C 131/1A was installed under the rear fuselage, but otherwise the armament corresponded to that of the R1. The R7 with a pressurised cabin was, like the A-2 and A-4 versions, only a design project.

Some He 177 A-6s were converted from A-3s and A-5s. The planned series version A-6/R1 had a four-gun tail position, a smaller bomb bay, and a pressure-tight canopy with removable armament. The maximum bomb load was 3,500kg. The He 177 A-6/R2 was intended to have a new cabin design and a remote-controlled lower nose position equipped with MG 131 Z machine guns. The forward dorsal position had an MG 151 Z, and the ventral position an MG 131. It was planned to mount one HDL 81 V manually-controlled rotary mount with four MG 131s in the tail.

A small series designated He 177 A-7, with DB 610 A/B engines and increased wing area, were adapted from the He 177 A-5 series. This variant's maximum bomb load was 4,200kg, and the defensive armament was considerably heavier than that of the A-6.

Heinkel considered producing the He 177 A-8, a bomber with four individual BMW 801 E engines, by converting He 177 A-5s. Later it was given the designation He 177 B-5. The He 177 A-10 was also equipped with four individual BMW 801 E engines, and the projected conversion of the He 177 A-7 was later given the designation He 177 B-7.

Below: The first unit to have He 177 bombers was I./Fernkampfgeschwader (Long-Range Bomber Group) 50, stationed at Zaporozhets.

The He 177 V 9 model, taken from the zero-series, was converted as He 177 B-5 with four individual engines, twin fins and rudders, and K-12 navigation equipment. In August 1944 the aircraft began flight tests at Rechlin. The V 101 (A-3), and V 102 (A-0) were also converted for the B-5 series, and in the same month these were test flown with single fins and rudders. The He 177 V 103 (A-5) after its conversion as 'He 177 B-5' had a manually-controlled four-gun mounting in the tail, and served as a flying test-bed for Heinkel-Süd at Wien-Schwechat, also in August 1944.

The prototype for the planned B-5 series, the He 177 V 104 (A-5), could not be manufactured at the time production was planned to begin in the summer of 1944. On 25 June 1944 the RLM cancelled the planned mass production of the He 177 B-5, and two weeks later the whole of the He 177 production was cancelled in favour of single-engined fighters and jet fighters such as the Me 262.

When production ceased in September 1944, some 1,146 aircraft (other than conversions), had been built since January 1942.

Below: For recovery of the heavy He 177, Heinkel designed its own equipment based on a half-track tractor.

Bottom: This He 177 A-5 (Works No.550060, KM+UJ) was attached to II./KG 40, and saw service over the Bay of Biscay.

Opposite page, top: An He 177 A-3 of KG 40. The rearmost dorsal position was fitted with an MG 131 as standard.

Opposite page, bottom: Aircraft of 4./KG 40 before the start of a training flight in south-west France.

Above: The last major units equipped with He 177 were those of I./KG 1 in the summer of 1944 on the Eastern Front.

Below: A squadron of He 177 A-5s of I./KG 100; an unusual view of German heavy bombers.

Opposite page, top: This He 177 A-3 of KG 40 was equipped with a special night-sight for the MG 151/20 installed in the tail position.

Opposite page, bottom: The HL 131 V tail position shown here was planned for the He 177 A-7, as well as for all He 177 B series aircraft.

Above: This He 177 A-5 (Works No.550054, KM+UD), still with its original markings, was attached to 6./KG 60.

Below: The last flying test-bed was the He 177 V 38 (A-5, KM+TB, Works No.550002). It was used for testing models with Fug 216 and 200 radars.

Bomber B

Opposite page, top: A drawing of the Ar E 340 with Jumo 222 radial engines. It was also planned to use two BMW 802s or DB 604s.

Opposite page, bottom: The E 340 had heavy defensive armament including this glazed twin-gun position fitted with either 20mm or 37mm cannon.

Right: One of several models of the Ju 288. Apart from the earlier cabin design, it shows twin Jumo 222 engines and a relatively small wingspan.

Right: This full-scale mock-up of the Ju 288 A-1 was viewed by representatives of the RLM on 15 December 1939.

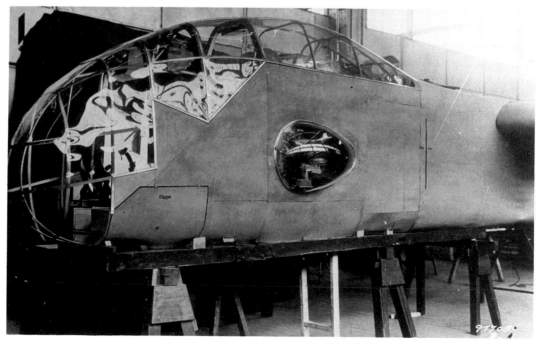

Junkers Ju 288

The Bomber B design was intended to replace the He 111 H and the Ju 88 A as the standard medium-range bomber. In July 1939 the RLM announced a competition for a successor to the previous medium bombers, and Arado, Dornier, Focke-Wulf and Junkers participated. The development division of the Junkers works at Dessau produced a design for a twin-engined high-altitude bomber with a three-seat pressurised cabin and remote-controlled defensive armament, powered by the Jumo 222 in-line engine. Dipl-Ing Heinrich Hertel, who from May 1939 was the company's Technical Director, was in charge of the design team. Representatives of the Technische Amt (Technical Division) of the RLM studied the full-scale mock-up of the pressurised cabin in December 1939, and after several modifications had been made, ordered the construction of a complete fuselage mock-up, which was approved by the RLM on 29 May 1940. A few days later, the

official order was received to build three prototypes with the designation Ju 288. However, Junkers had already begun construction of the prototypes in February 1940 on their own initiative, so production was already under way.

Junkers fitted a Ju 288 canopy and twin fins and rudders to the Ju 88 V 2 and V 7, and began flight testing of these components in early 1940. On 29 November 1940 the Ju 288 V 1 (D-AACS, Works No.0001) made its maiden flight after extensive ground testing. Because the Jumo 222 was not yet ready for mass production, the V 1 was initially flown with two BMW 801 radial engines. The Ju 288 V 2 (BG+GR), which had modified dive-brakes, was delivered for flight testing on 29 November 1940, and the third prototype (BG+GS?), again with BMW 801s, was delivered on 18 April 1941.

The flying qualities of the aircraft were unsatisfactory, and a fuselage extension of

Right: By the early autumn of 1940 the Ju 288 V1 was already in an advanced stage of construction. Guards were fitted to protect the side sighting positions.

Right: The Ju 288 V 1 (D-AACS) made its first flight on 29 November 1940, but was lost on 2 March 1941.

Left: The Ju 88 V 5 (D-ATYU) served as the test aircraft for the development of the Ju 288.

99262

Left: The third Ju 288 test aircraft (DG+GS) was manufactured a little later and flew for the first time on 18 April 1941. It was stood down in October 1943 in Giessen.

Below: Twin Jumo 222s powered the Ju 288 V 9 (VE+QP), which made its first flight on 6 April 1942, though they were still unreliable engines at the time.

almost a metre was necessary. Furthermore, the landing gear proved to be weak. The Ju 288 V 4 (BG+GT), completed in 1941, had no dive-brakes because the heavy dive-bomber role was no longer considered necessary. It made its first flight on 17 May that year. Two years later, on 18 October 1943, it was transferred to Tarnewitz. The Ju 288 V 5 served as the first test bed for the more powerful Jumo 222 A/B and, owing to delays in delivering the new engines, V 5's first flight did not take place until 8 October 1941, V 6 following on 18 January 1942. Both of these aircraft had greater wing area, with the wing span increased to 22.67m, and were finally stood down by Junkers in October 1943.

The Ju 288 V 8 (RD+MN) served as a weapons test aircraft, and the ninth machine first flew in May 1943, powered by Jumo 222 C/Ds. The Ju 288 V 11 (DF+CO), which flew for the first time on 21 July 1942, was used to test the more powerful but heavier DB 606 A/B high-altitude engines.

Also in early 1942, the seventh test aircraft had to be flown with two BMW 801 C radial engines because the Jumo 222 A/B was still not yet available. During the course of

repair after an engine fire, a larger tail unit was fitted. This machine, too, ceased flying at the end of 1943.

Although several different series of the Ju 288 were planned, only one was actually produced. The Ju 288 A series was designed with a 22m wingspan, and the A-1 was intended to have a large, all-round-vision gun position at the side of the nose, without a periscope sight. The planned A-2 version was to have a faired, side-mounted remotely controlled nose gun barbettes with a periscope sight. Its take-off weight was to be 18,500kg, giving a maximum bomb load of 5,000kg. Since the Technische Amt had, in the meantime, decided on a four-crew cabin design, the planned series was abandoned in favour of the Ju 288 B-1 with the enlarged cabin and a new wing. The prototype was mothballed.

The B series had the Ju 288 A fuselage, with a somewhat wider forward section, and increased wingspan. The defensive armament consisted of remote-controlled MG 131 machine guns mounted in the nose and in a dorsal turret behind the pressurised cabin. In the tail gun position it was intended to have twin MG 131s, one MG 151/15, or one MG

Below: The pressurised cabin planned for the Ju 288 A-1 under construction. The forward section of the fuselage was later used in one of the test aircraft.

Above: Full-scale mock-up of the four-seat cabin. Because of problems with the Jumo 222 double radial engine, two DB 610s were now used.

Left: A loading test with an SB 2500. This heavy bomb had a length of 3.69m and a diameter of 0.78m.

Above right: The Ju 288 V 11 (DF+CQ) was also powered by the Jumo 222 high-performance engine, and made its maiden flight on 21 July 1942.

Right: The Ju 288 V 13 (DF+CS) crashed on 15 May 1943

Left: The first Ju 288 V 101 (the first C-1) undergoes an engine test in early 1943 at Dessau.

151/20, also remotely-controlled. To reduce all-up weight, the bomb load was limited to 3,600kg. The V 9 aircraft was used as prototype for the B series, and in March 1944 it was at the Junkers plant at Dessau.

As the Jumo 222 was not going to be available in sufficient quantities in the foreseeable future, the Ju 288 was eventually fitted with two DB 606 A/B engines, with which the eleventh test model was flight tested. In this version, designated Ju 288 C-1, the canopy was extended by 0.33m and the airframe was strengthened. In addition, a ventral gun position aft of the bomb bay was envisaged. The first prototypes for this series were the Ju 288 V 101 and V 102, which were flight tested in August 1942 with DB 606 A/B engines. On 5 November 1943 a presentation was made at Dessau to Generalfeldmarschall Göring. Eleven days later another presentation was made at Rastenberg to Hitler himself. The Ju 288 V 103 to 108 were powered by DB 610 A/B engines as an interim solution. Up to the end of October 1943, Works Nos. 310151 to 310155 were assembled.

On 4 December 1943 the first Ju 288 C-1 (Works No. 310151) made its maiden test flight with test pilot Holzbaur at the controls. However, at the beginning of 1944 the RLM cancelled the entire series and all further development after only 21 test aircraft had been built.

Left: Tests of the first Ju 288 C-1 took place at the Dessau works at the end of 1943.

Dornier Do 317

Like the Ju 288, the Do 317 was seen as a future 'Bomber B'. In fact, Dornier brought an improved Do 217 K-1 up to the specification standard in 1939. The full-scale mock-up followed in the summer of 1940, and on 17 October 1940 it was viewed by representatives of the Rechlin and Tarnewitz Research Establishments and the RLM. Any of the high-altitude engines available, the DB 603, DB 604, Jumo 222 or BMW 802, were regarded as suitable powerplants. In December 1940 there were, in addition to the Do 317 A-1 (with Jumo 222 engines), a further two designs using the DB 603, and these were presented to the Technische Amt in Berlin as part of the pro-

ject outline. These versions, which lacked pressurised cockpits, were followed by the Do 317B, a multi-seat bomber with a pressurised cockpit and wingspan increased to 26m. At the end of the design phase the Do 317 was given two Jumo 222 engines and greatly improved defensive armament. This consisted of one MG 81 Z in the nose and a heavier MG 151/20 in the lower nose for defence against attack from below. In addition the aircraft had dorsal and ventral positions, both equipped with MG 131s. The bomb bay was larger than that of the Do 217, and could now take up to four SC 1000s, eight SC 500s, any of the currently available bombs, or four BSB 700 bomb racks. In gen-

Left: The Do 317 V 1 resembled the planned A-1 series in most details. Many variants, especially a high-altitude bomber with a pressurised cabin and greater wingspan, were under development.

eral, the Do 317 was only slightly larger than the Do 217 K, but had a more spacious fuselage because of its greater cross-sectional area. The most obvious difference lay in the triangular rudders of the Do 217 M-9.

On 12 November 1941 the Technische Amt permitted the use of the DB 610 double engine, since production of the Jumo 222 had not yet begun. Dornier, Focke-Wulf and Junkers were required to make provision for using all engines currently available.

The first of six prototypes of the Do 317 flew on 8 September 1943, powered by DB 603 Bs. However, because the new high-altitude engines were required for the main production series of the Ju 188, further development of the Do 317 was stopped, and in 1943 the components of the V 2 aircraft which had been completed were scrapped. All planned variants were cancelled.

Focke-Wulf Fw 191

Opposite page, bottom: A cabin mock-up for the planned Fw 191 A-1 series, summer 1941.

Below: The Fw 191 V 1 under construction at the end of 1941.

The third competitor for a series order in the 'Bomber B' programme was the four-seat Focke-Wulf Fw 191. This was designed for two Jumo 222 C/D or two DB 610 A/B double engines, and its estimated maximum speed was in excess of 600km/h and the operational ceiling over 10,000m. With a flying weight of 26,650kg, it was intended to carry a 6,000kg bomb load, including LT 1500 aerial torpedoes as well as all current types of bomb. The Fw 191 A-1's defensive armament consisted of two MG 151 machine guns on twin mounts in the nose and tail, plus two remote-controlled MG 81 Zs in the rear of the engine nacelles.

At the same time the RLM issued a research requirement stating that the Fw 191 should have all hydraulic and mechanical systems operated by electric servo-motors. For this reason the aircraft was humorously known as the 'flying power-station'.

Owing to problems with the new Class II engines (Jumo 222 and DB 604) in the autumn

Opposite page, top: At the beginning of 1942, only the Fw 191 V 1 and V 2 models were available for testing the proposed Bomber B.

Opposite page, bottom: Dipl-Ing Kosel was test pilot of the BMW 801 MA-powered Fw 191 V 1.

Above: Even during works testing of the Fw 191 V 1 there were many breakdowns.

Below: The Fw 191 V 2 was also powered by two BMW 801 MA engines, since once again the Jumo 222 was not available.

of 1940, the design section had to work with the less-powerful BMW 801, which meant that the anticipated performance could no longer be achieved.

In the winter of 1941 the Technische Amt permitted the Fw 191 X13 project to proceed with manually-controlled gun positions with MG 131 machine guns, because the remotely-controlled units were not yet suitable for mass production.

At the beginning of 1942 Dipl-Ing Mehlhorn was able to take the Fw 191 V 1 on its first flight at Hannover Langenhagen, with BMW 801 MA engines providing the power. After the RLM had cancelled the Fw 191 V 3 to V 5 prototypes, there remained the V 6 which, at the end of 1942, was fitted with a pair of Jumo 222 A/Bs. This flew for the first time in early 1943 at Delmenhorst, near Bremen, with Flug Kapitän Hans Sander at the controls.

The first two test machines logged no flying hours because the electrical servo-motors were prone to breakdowns and the multi-sectioned combined landing flap and dive brake, called the 'Multhopp-Klappe' after its designer, Hans Multhopp, was prone to flutter. The third test aircraft, the Fw 191 V 6, had some of its electrics replaced by hydraulic systems to enable flight testing to proceed without constant interruptions.

As with the Ju 288 and Do 317, Focke-Wulf intended that the Fw 191 B should have DB 606 or DB 610 double engines. However, this variant was not built, and neither was the unpressurised Fw 191 C, which was intended to have four single Jumo 211 F, DB 601 E, DB 605, or DB 628 engines. Mass production of the Fw 191 was abandoned because of work on the Ju 388 K and L series.

Development of the unconventional twin-boom Arado Ar E 340 never went ahead.

Below: The first installation of the Jumo 222 A/B was in the Fw 191 V 6. For the V 2, seen here, Dipl-Ing Mehlron had to manage with the less powerful BMW 801 MA.

High-Speed Bombers

Right: An Me 210 A-1 of Test Squadron 210, which eventually became III./Heavy-Fighter Group.

Below: A monthly output of 100 Ju 88 S-1s was planned for November 1943, to meet the demands of bomber groups in the West.

Heinkel He 70

The German airline Luft Hansa needed an airliner to compete with America's high-speed Lockheed Orion, and in response to the requirement Siegfried Günter began development of the Heinkel He 65 in 1931. It soon became clear, however, that the Orion's performance would not be matched by the He 65, so Heinkel embarked on a completely new design. On 14 June 1932 the building specification for the He 70 was issued, and a fortnight later detail construction began. The first flight followed on 1 December 1932. The fuselage and wings had been considerably improved, and a retractable undercarriage, flush rivets and streamlined cabin glazing gave a significant increase in speed compared with the He 65.

On 22 March 1933 the He 70 set one of several international records, covering 1,000km at an average speed of 347km/h while carrying a 500kg load. On 26 April the same year it attained a maximum speed of 377km/h. This performance could be improved still further with more powerful engines, and when Rolls-Royce bought an He 70 and installed a Kestrel V, a speed of 415km/h was attained. With a Peregrine I (the Kestrel's successor) the aircraft achieved a speed of 481km/h at an altitude of 5,075m in October 1938.

The He 70 offered the Luftwaffe the possibility of rapidly acquiring a high-speed bomber and reconnaissance aircraft which could clearly outperform even current fighters. The required modifications were therefore made at the beginning of 1934.

The original asymmetric cockpit was widened, the rear of the cabin was converted to an open machine-gun position, and a bomb bay was provided. By the end of 1934, in addition to the converted prototype He 70 C (D-UHYS),

the Luftwaffe had a further eleven He 70 Cs and nine He 70 Ds. These versions served as courier aircraft, and represented an intermediate stage in the development of the military He 70 E and F.

A high-speed light bomber, the He 70 E had three vertical bomb magazines for six 50kg bombs. The series was delivered to the Luftwaffe in early 1935, and a little while later the long-range-reconnaissance He 70 F went into service.

In November 1936 reconnaissance squadron A/88 of the Condor Legion in Spain was equipped with eighteen He 70 F-2s, and these were often used for armed reconnaissance. However, the design's low-set, deep-chord wing obscured the observer's downward view and restricted the field of fire of the rear gun. Moreover, the enclosed, flat-topped cabin further impeded observation and made the rapid identification of targets difficult. In addition, the wooden wings were considered a fire risk. The aircraft were eventually replaced by the Do 17 F, and twelve He 70s were transferred to the Spanish Nationalist air force.

Hungary received eighteen He 170s (a version powered by a Gnome-Rhone engine) in 1937/38, and in June 1941 these, too, were used for reconnaissance, despite their deficiencies in this role.

By April 1937 the Luftwaffe had abandoned plans to use the He 70 as a production aircraft, and retained it for the Civil Reserve. In September 1939 the type was no longer on the complement of serving units. The auxiliary reconnaissance version was transferred from long-range reconnaissance groups to training centres, aerial photography schools, and courier squadrons.

Right: The He 70 E-1 was planned as a high-speed auxiliary bomber.

Right: The Hs 124 V 2 three-seat high-speed bomber and fighter-bomber. Because it was underpowered, there was no chance of mass production.

Messerschmitt Bf 162

In the summer of 1934 the RLM received a memorandum from Willy Messerschmitt and Robert Luser of the Bayerische Flugzeug-Werke (BFW — later to become the Messerschmitt works), in which Project P 1035 was described. Using a modular design principle, a heavy fighter (later the Bf 110), a high-altitude reconnaissance aircraft (later the Bf 161), and a bomber (later the Bf 162) were to be developed. For each variant a specially adapted fuselage would be used. The RLM took up the proposal and issued successive orders for all three types. Development of the Bf 161 began almost in parallel with that of the Bf 110 in September 1934. Work on the Bf 162 was concluded a year later, and in November 1935 BFW issued the technical requirements for the high-speed bomber. At the same time the RLM was carrying out its initial examination of the model of the long-range-reconnaissance Bf 161 at Augsburg. The basic application of the Bf 162 as a high-speed bomber was then emphasised after certain modifications had been carried out.

Construction of the Bf 162 began in January 1936, and later in the year five test aircraft were produced. A total of 65 production aircraft was included in the financial programme for 1937/38.

On 26 February 1937 the Bf 162 V 1 (D-AIXA, Works No.817) made its first flight, piloted by Dr H. Wurster. It was powered by two DB 600 D engines, and had a flying weight of 6,500kg. The V 2 (D-AOBE, Works No.818) flew for the first time on 31 October 1937, and the V 3 (D-AOVI, Works No.819) on 7 July 1938. However, four months previously, on 9 March 1938, the high speed bomber programme had been cancelled in favour of the Ju 88. At this point the Bf 162, with its top speed of 500km/h, was faster than the Bf 109 D. The interruption of the programme was necessitated by the RLM's choice of emphasis in aircraft production. As the RLM explained, although the performance of the Bf 162 exceeded that of the Ju 88, BFW was already committed to development of the Bf 109 and Bf 110 as well as new fighters, and for that reason they had chosen the Ju 88 for mass production.

Materials obtained for the construction of further Bf 162 test aircraft were easily absorbed into the production of Bf 110 Cs because of the original modular design concept. The Bf 162 V 1 was scrapped. The second prototype served for a while as a tug for the Me 163 rocket fighter project. After a photographic sortie with the Bf 162, pictures of the aircraft were retouched for propaganda purposes to show the aircraft as the new Messerschmitt Jaguar heavy fighter for use against England in early 1940. The Bf 162 V 3 was transferred to the Rechlin Research Centre in 1939.

Above: An unsuccessful competitor to the Ju 88 A-1 was the three-seat high-speed Bf 161 V 2 (D-AOFI).

Below: The Bf 162 was intended as a high-speed bomber and reconnaissance aircraft. The V 2 model seen here (D-AOBE) was powered by two DB 600 A engines.

Arado Ar 240 and Ar 440

Dipl-Ing Walter Blume, the Technical Director of Arado Flugzeugbau, offered the RLM the company's Project E 240, a twin-engined 'heavy fighter-bomber' with remotely-controlled streamlined gun positions with periscopic sights, and in early 1938 the RLM issued an order for several prototypes. On 10 May 1940 the Ar 240 V 1 made its maiden flight, to be followed two months later by the V 2. Unfortunately, both aircraft exhibited poor stability in all axes. These problems were partly resolved in the third aircraft (KK+CD) by increasing the wing area and lengthening the fuselage. This machine was the first Ar 240 intended for dive-bombing and reconnaissance.

Owing to the small fuselage cross-section, the bomb load had to be carried under the wings. In the late summer, after extensive flight testing and modification, the V 3 flew with Aufklärungsgruppe des Oberbefehlshabers der Luftwaffe (Aufklgr. ObdL). The Ar 240 V 4 was intended primarily for the dive-bomber role, and had eight ETC 50s under the wings. However, since the aircraft proved unsuited to this role, the succeeding zero-series aircraft were conceived as reconnaissance aircraft (V 5 to V 8), a heavy fighter (V 9), and a night-fighter (V 10). The Ar 240 V 11 and V 12 (C-03 and C-04) were designed as heavy fighter-bombers and could carry a 1,800kg

Below: Maintenance work on the Ar 240 V 6. The Ar 240 was the forerunner of the Ar 440 and was to be used for reconnaissance as well as for offensive purposes.

bomb load. To improve performance, a GM-1 injection system was fitted.

Although the Ar 240 was aerodynamically excellent and had a good performance, plans for mass production were dropped at the end of 1942 by the RLM in favour of the Me 210. Consequently, none of the proposed series – the Ar 240 C-1 heavy fighter-bomber with the DB 603 G engine, the C-2 night-fighter, and the Ar 240 C-3 and C-4 high-speed bomber and reconnaissance variants – nor their further development, the Ar 240 E, was produced.

The Ar 440 was an improved development of the Ar 240. The first prototype of this heavy fighter-bomber was cleared to fly in the early summer of 1942. The three following Ar 440 A-0s flew for the first time in November 1942, and in the following January they were sent to the Test Centre at Rechlin. Among other tests, comparative flight testing with the Ju 88 S, Me 410 and He 219 high-speed bombers was undertaken, and the Ar 440 showed considerable advantages in both speed and flying qualities. Further flight tests were even more convincing, so the Technische Amt issued an order for series production of the Ar 440. However, in the fighter programme of 1944 the Do 335 replaced the Ar 440, and further development was stopped.

The Ar 440 A-0 had two DB 603 G engines, a heavy forward armament of two MK 108 cannon and two MG 151/20 machine guns, two MG 131s in remotely-controlled barbettes in the fuselage, a rearward firing MG 151/20, and could carry a 1,000kg bomb load. Its maximum speed was 750km/h at 11,000m.

Right: A drawing of the Ar 440 high-speed bomber with external bomb racks.

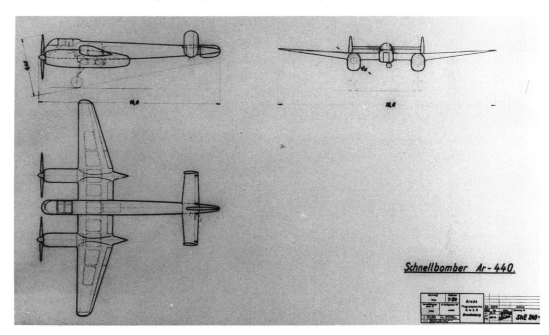

Schnellbomber Ar-440.

Right: The Ar 240 V 6 (T9+GL) was flown as a fast reconnaissance aircraft by OLt Horst Götz (ObdL Reconnaissance Group).

Messerschmitt Me 410

Above: The Me 210 A-1 provided effective support to the single-engined fighter-bombers of the Luftwaffe, thanks to its 1,350hp DB 601 engines.

Left: A close-up of the remotely-controlled mounting with a rear-ward firing MG 131, as fitted to the flanks of both the Me 210 and Me 410 bombers.

Above: Test models V 18 and V 22 were used for armament and bomb testing for the Me 410 A-1 series.

The Me 410 (by this time the Bayerische Flugzeug-Werke had abandoned the Bf prefix in favour of Me, for Messerschmitt) could not fully meet the requirements for a high-speed bomber, and, like the multi-role Me 210, displayed poor flying characteristics. It was for this reason that, in 1942, two-and-a-half years after the first flight of the Me 210 V 1 (2 September 1939), mass production of the type had been halted.

In March 1942 Messerschmitt tested the Me 210 V 17 with a new, extended tail section. These tests showed acceptable flying properties, and at the end of April Göring cancelled the halt in production so that the Me 210 with the more powerful DB 603 engine and the modified fuselage could be produced as the Me 410. In the autumn of 1942 the Me 410 V 1, a converted Me 210 A, made its first test flight.

From the first prototypes arose the high-speed bomber Me 410 A-1, which in January 1943 went into mass production at Augsburg. With the Me 410 V 5 Lotfe bomb sight installation followed. The two-seater Me 410 had the DB 603 A-1 engine (some with GM-1 injection systems), which gave it a maximum speed of 615km/h. The flying weight was 11,240kg,

which included a 1,000kg bomb load carried in the bomb bay. With full fuel tanks only a single SD/SC 500 bomb could be carried, but it was possible to retrofit racks for four SC 50 bombs in tandem under the wings. Alternatively, an extra fuel tank could be carried in the bomb bay. Armament consisted of two fixed MG 151/20s and MG 17s in the nose, and as defensive armament the high-speed bomber had two rearward-firing MG 131 machine-guns in remote-controlled barbettes on either side of the fuselage.

Up to the end of 1943, 457 Me 410 As had been produced by the Augsburg factory, and the type partly replaced the Do 217 Es with KG 2.

When the Me 410 was used with the GM-1 injection system it had an endurance of only 66 minutes. In June 1943 the Me 410 V 13 was subjected to performance testing at Rechlin, when it reached a speed of 580km/h at 6,500m. In September a further test programme was carried out with improved GM-1 injection systems.

Three variants were planned, one being a single-seater with fixed MG 151/20 machine-guns and capable of carrying one SC 500

bomb. With the U1 conversion kit the Me 410 A-1 became an auxiliary reconnaissance aircraft, and the A-1/U2 was used as an auxiliary heavy fighter. The Me 410 A-1 was manufactured by Dornier as well as by Messerschmitt. In April 1944 production of the Me 410 B-1 was transferred entirely from Messerschmitt to Dornier. The high-speed bomber differed from the A-series in having the more powerful DB 603 G engine of 1,900hp (1,400kW).

In early 1944 several Me 410 B-6s with FuG 200 search radar served as anti-ship aircraft, operating from Lorient in France. They were equipped with two MG 131s and, as standard equipment, the WB 103 (twin MK 103 cannon). The Me 410 B-5 torpedo bomber did not come through the testing stage. Using at least three aircraft (DI+NF, PP+VG, and SH+NY), aerial torpedo tests and tests with

rolling bombs such as the 'Kurt', were carried out in the autumn of 1944.

On 1 July 1944, production of the Me 410 was cancelled in favour of the emergency fighter programme. However, the OKL had already decided to convert the Me 410 from a high-speed bomber to a heavy fighter. Production of the reconnaissance series therefore continued, although planned development of an Me 410 with one or two Jumo 004 jet engines, and also of a high-altitude version, was cancelled.

Production by Messerschmitt at Regensburg and Augsburg and by Dornier at Oberpfaffenhofen totalled 1,160 aircraft. The first to fall victim to the RAF was 2H+CA of Research Squadron 210, on 6 September 1942. The last Me 410 claimed by the RAF, 9K+HP of 6./KG 51, was shot down on 13 June 1944.

Above: The internal bomb bay could carry up to eight SC 50 bombs, two SC 250s, or two SC 500s.

Heinkel He 119

The paired-engine layout as used in the He 177 had already been approved by Siegfried Günter in the 1930s and by General Wever for the He 119 high-speed bomber. In this case, two DB 601 A engines were coupled to form a DB 606 A-1 double engine, and installed in the centre of the fuselage. From there it drove a nose-mounted four-bladed propeller of 4.3m diam-eter via a long shaft which extended through the extensively glazed cockpit. On 22 November 1937 the He 119 V 4 set a world speed record of 505km/h over 1,000km carrying a 1,000kg payload (all-up weight 8,000kg). Altogether Heinkel built eight He 119s, but the Luftwaffe decided against mass production.

The He 119 V 3 was fitted with floats, and the He 119 V 7 and V 8 were eventually delivered to Japan.

Below: Designed as a lightly-armed, two-seat high-speed bomber, the He 119 was powered by a DB 606 A-2 double engine.

Above: The engines of the He 119 V 4 (D-ANTE) were tested for a record attempt in December 1937.

Junkers Ju 88 S

Opposite page, bottom: Production of Ju 88 S-1s fell well behind schedule: in May 1944, for instance, only nine aircraft were produced, which was insufficient to cover the requirements of KG 6 and 66.

Below: This Ju 88 S-3 was delivered directly to I./KG 6 by a crew (DLH) of Aircraft Transfer Group 1.

The Ju 88 S was a modification of the Ju 88 A to suit the aircraft to the more stringent requirements of the aerial war in western Europe. The first prototype Ju 88 S (Ju 88 V 55) made its first flight on 28 December 1942. The second prototype, Ju 88 V 56, was followed by a small Ju 88 S-0 series. The aircraft mainly resembled the Ju 88 A-4, but lacked the ventral turret and dive brakes. In place of the glass nose panels of earlier aircraft, the Ju 88 S had a smooth, hemispherical glazed nose. The complete defensive armament consisted solely of a rearwards firing MG 131, and it could carry a 1,000kg bomb load. The power of the BMW 801 C/D engines could be enhanced by add-on GM-1 fuel injection equipment. With this and with some aerodynamic improvements, the Ju 88 S reached a maximum speed of 600km/h.

With the Ju 88 S-1 the BMW 801 D radial engine was used. This series corresponded almost exactly with the zero-series, and up to December 1943 some 50 aircraft had been built.

The Ju 88 S-2 series was already under way in June 1943. This pathfinder aircraft had the large wooden bomb bay on the planned Ju 88 A-15, but after a test model had been manufactured no further production took place.

Above: Crash landing of a Ju 88 S-3 of Bomber Group 6 at Montdidier.

Below: Another crew of Aircraft Transfer Group 1 with a Ju 88 S-3 which had landed in the neighbourhood of Holzhausen in Bavaria.

The Ju 88 S-3 high-speed bomber was equipped with two Jumo 213 engines and was intended to replace the S-2. Up to March 1944 about 70 were delivered. The bomb load was 2,000kg.

The Ju 88 S-4, a converted S-3 with enlarged wooden bomb-bay, remained a development project. The TK-11 turbocharger was used in the S-5 series. Two prototypes, Ju 88 V 93 and V 94, were flight tested, but the cost of the supercharger was the reason that mass production was cancelled in 1944. According to service records, nine Ju 88 Ss were serving with Luftflotte 3 in May 1944, while 99 were delivered in June and July and a further 74 in August.

In September 1944 twelve Ju 88 S-3s became available. They served with pathfinder training schools, the Head of TLR, KG 66, Erg. Grp. KG 66, and Flight Transfer Groups.

Below: Many Ju 88 S-3s were stationed in Aalborg, Deelen, Montdidier, and Soesterberg from August 1943.

Dornier Do 335

The Dornier Do 335 arose from a high-speed bomber specification of 28 September 1942. On 16 January 1943 the RLM issued the first order, and model-viewing took place on 18 April 1943. The prototype of the twin-engined high-speed bomber (CP+UA, Works No.230001) flew for the first time on 26 October 1943, piloted by Flugkapitän Hans Dieterle at Mengen/Württ.

The role of the Do 335 changed during the course of the war. In November 1943 the high-speed bomber variant was given priority over the heavy fighter, the night fighter, or the reconnaissance aircraft. In January 1944 this order was reversed. The RLM now required the reconnaissance version to be given priority, followed by the heavy fighter, high-speed bomber and night fighter. At the end of March 1944 the order came to hold up the bomber version and accelerate production of the Do 335 as a heavy fighter, yet only three months later the Do 335 A-1 and A-2 were produced as bombers. At the beginning of August 1944 production of the A-3 reconnaissance aircraft was replaced by the A-6 night fighter. Again, only two months elapsed before, on 26 September 1944, even development of the night fighter was dropped, so that the emphasis could be placed on the heavy fighter. On 10 October the Luftwaffe changed its mind yet again, and ordered the series as a night fighter. On 15 November 1944 the prototype (Do 335 A-6) became available, although not as a night fighter.

After tests at Mengenn/Würff and Friedrichshafen, trials of the Do 335 at Rechlin followed immediately, using two prototypes and two zero-series aircraft. Up to the end of February 1945, however, only incomplete results had been obtained.

Right: Only a few Do 335s remained intact at the end of the war. This one, the A-05, was discovered at Lechfeld in April 1945.

Right: A considerable number of loading trials were carried out on a zero-series aircraft (Do 335 A-0). Here, an SC 500 bomb is loaded in the bomb bay.

Left: The Do 335 was designed in reconnaissance, night-fighter and heavy-fighter versions, as well as its high speed bomber form. The first prototype (CP+UA) flew on 26 October 1943.

The Do 335 had some novel features, such as an ejector seat and a nosewheel. Fourteen test aircraft and nine pre-series aircraft (Do 335 A-0) were followed by five aircraft with dual control and tandem seats. The A-3 auxiliary reconnaissance version, planned in the autumn of 1944, as well as the A-4 unarmed long-range reconnaissance version and the A-8 and A-9 reconnaissance versions, were never produced.

The Do 335 A-1 fighter-bomber was produced from September 1944 at Oberpfaffenhofen. The powerplant consisted of two DB 603 E 1 engines each of 1,802hp (1,325kW). Later, an MW 40 methanol-water injection system was added to increase power. The aircraft could carry 500kg bombs in the bomb bay and two SC 250s on external bomb racks. Armament consisted of one MK 103 cannon firing through the propeller spinner, and two MG 151s in the upper fuselage.

At the end of February 1945 the Do 335 was forced to give way to the Ta 152 and the Me 262. Because of serious hold-ups in development, the Do 335 had only a small speed advantage over the Ta 152, and its endurance was no better. Moreover, its fuel consumption was too great, and production and repair costs were too high. A variant of the Do 335 with Jumo 004 or HeS 011 jet engines was dropped in 1944.

Apart from the Do 335, Dornier also developed the Do 435 A-1 and A-2, which were bombers with twin DB 603 LA engines, larger wings, and, in the latter case, a pressurised cabin. There was also the Do 435 D-1 (with enlarged wings) and D-2 (with pressurised cabin). Both projects were intended to be powered by the DB 603 L-2 engine.

Messerschmitt Me 262

Plans for a high-speed bomber based on the Me 262 pursuit fighter were prepared in early 1943. An initial bomb carrier was tested on the Me 262 V 10 between April 1943 and April 1944. From 10 June 1944 the emergency programme for the Me 262 'Blitzbomber' was in progress at Rechlin. However, four days previously, on 6 June 1944, the invasion of Europe had begun, and the Normandy landings were already in the past when training of pilots of 3./KG 51 began at Lechfeld on 20 June.

The high-speed blitzbomber differed from the fighter version of the Me 262 in having 'Wiking Schiffer' ('Viking Ship') bomb racks and additional fuel tanks, and in other minor airframe modifications. However, once again, production difficulties delayed the advent of the jet bomber. The official requirement that the aircraft should have a minimum flying altitude of 4,000m over enemy territory was an unreasonable objective. The very small numbers of Blitzbombers produced meant that they

Left: The Deutsche Forschungsanstalt für Segelflug (DFS - German Sailplane Research Institute) developed an air trailer for the V 1, as well as for 500kg and 1,000kg loads and a 900lit drop tank.

Left: The Me 262 V 10 (pilot Gerd Lindner) towed an empty container on 30 October 1944, and on 18 November carried an SC 500 bomb.

Right: As early as 28 May 1944 it had been decided that the Me 262 A should be urgently developed an a Blitzbomber. The aircraft shown was classed as an auxiliary blitzbomber of Type A-1a/Bo.

Right: The Me 262 A-2a was first attached to Erprobungskommando Edelweiss and later to I./KG 51.

Below: The Me 262 A-1a/Bo and A-2a usually flew with two SC 500 bombs, or AB 250 drop tanks and one SC 500 or one AB 500 in the West.

could only attack individually, although up to 10 April 1945 KG 51 had been supplied with 342 Me 262s.

When the 'Kommando Edelweiss', as EKdo 51 was known, arrived at Chateaudun on 20 July 1944, only four serviceable Me 262s were available. On 28 August 1944 seven Blitzbombers, most equipped with AB 500 bomb racks carrying a full load of SD 10 bombs, flew from Juvincourt on four sorties against Allied troop positions. At the end of August only twenty bombs were available, so they had to revert to SC 250 bombs.

The Allied advance led to bomber squadrons being moved back to Belgium at the end of August 1944, and later to Volkel-Eindhoven in Holland. Then, on 4 September 1944, the base was subject to a heavy attack by the RAF, and the jet bomber command retreated still further to Rheine/Westfalen. From there it was mainly the Liege area that was attacked. At the end of September the bridges at Nijmegen and airfields at Chievres, Eindhoven, Nijmegen and Volkel were attacked using SD 250 demolition bombs and AB 250 anti-personnel bombs. By mid-November 1944 the pilots of KG 51 had achieved an incredible accuracy of within 100m in horizontal attack.

On 20 November 1944, I./KG 51 had a total of 28 Me 262s, the second group at Schwäbisch-Hall had only fifteen, and the third group fewer than fourteen. In the first six days after the beginning of the 'Battle of the Bulge' on 16 December 1944, the Blitzbombers flew their first long-range attacks on targets in the snowbound Ardennes. At the end of 1944 'Operation Bodenplatte' was in various phases of preparation. Early in the morning of New Year's Day 1945, Blitzbombers of I./KG 51 attacked a number of airfields in the Brussels, Arnhem, Eindhoven, and Venlo areas. To cover their own retreat, the OKL ordered on 13 February 1945 that 'the main units of the moving war should be attacked with bombs and on-board armament by day using jet aircraft, and by night using night-fighter groups at the front line'. The first jet bomber attacks on the bridges at Remagen followed on 7 March. Several attacks were carried out, but with little result. However, the bridge collapsed after American ground forces had been using it for a few days.

On 13 March 1945 the 'General authorised by the Führer for jet aircraft', Waffen-SS General Dr Kammler, ordered that KG 51 should come within IX.Fliegerkorps under the command of General Kammhuber, and thenceforth be used for the defence of the Reich. At the beginning of April the Me 262s were brought together into another group. At that time JG 7 had about fifteen, KG(J) 51 about 41, the Kommando Stamp had five, the General of Reconnaissance Aircraft had three, and the KdE one. Of the 342 Blitzbombers built, 88 were lost through enemy action and 146 through technical defects or by being sent away for training purposes. From mid-April 1945 new replacements promised to the units could no longer be delivered.

Above: Training to load an Me 262 A-1a with two SC 250 bombs.

New targets could now only be engaged in the Würzburg region. On 2 April 1945 the majority of II./KG 51 at Straßkirchen was captured by tanks of the US Seventh Army. On 30 April seven Me 262s retreated from Riem to Hörsching, and one day later to Prague-Rusin. The remainder of II./KG 51 was captured on 29 April 1945 by the US XXth Corps.

The two-crew Me 262 A-2a/U2, which was to have the TSA bombsight as standard, with a prone position for the bomb aimer in the nose, only reached the prototype stage because of the approaching end of the war. Nevertheless, some towing tests did take place. Plans for an improved jet bomber based on the Me 262 came to nothing.

Left: A parked Me 262 A-2 Blitzbomber, already loaded up with two bombs.

The Lippisch Project

Alexander Lippisch had begun to test flying-wing gliders as early as 1921, and in the 1930s the construction of the 'Delta' glider followed. From this arose the later DFS 194 design, and pursuance of the tailless aircraft concept resulted in the Me 163 of 1940, the world's first mass-produced rocket powered aircraft. Because of this design, the 'L Division' of Messerschmitt was set up in 1939 under the leadership of Professor Lippisch to investigate further advanced designs. Aircraft under consideration included a twin-engined trainer (P 04-114), a rocket-propelled fighter-bomber (P 09),

and a jet fighter (P 010), as well as the P 08 four-engined heavy-bomber (September 1941), and the P 11 high-speed bomber.

The L Division P 04 design series produced the Me 329 high-speed bomber and heavy fighter design in August 1942. This twin-engined aircraft with pusher propellers and a nosewheel undercarriage could carry as its maximum load one SC 1000 bomb. At least four machine guns were available as fixed forward armament. From the Me 329, the P 10 heavy fighter design, later designated Me 265, was developed. Part of the Me 210's fuselage

Below: A full-scale mock-up of the Me 329 high-speed bomber and heavy fighter. It had a wing span of 17.5m and a length of only 8.55m.

was to be incorporated in this tailless aircraft, which, like the Me 329, had swept back wings and pusher propellers. Both projects were intended for comparative testing with the Me 410, and reached the model design stage.

The P 11, in its initial form as a two-seat, high-speed flying-wing bomber, was tested on 13 September 1942 with two jet engines housed in the wing roots. The second design (2 December 1942) was a single-seat high-speed bomber with adjustable stabilisers built into the fixed faces of the rudders which were hydraulically operated to move in the horizontal plane.

This was intended to give the aircraft a higher coefficient of lift, which was a requirement of tailless aircraft. The P 11 could carry one SC 1000 bomb and had a fuel capacity of 2,200kg.

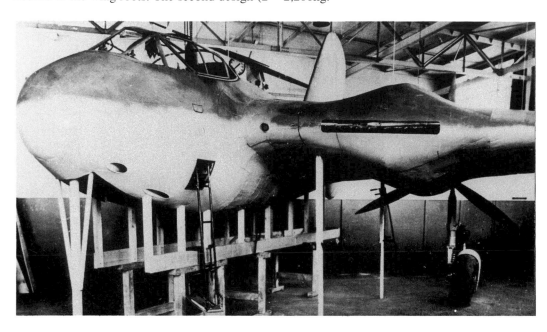

Left: The two-seat Me 329 A-1 had four fixed 20mm or 30mm machine guns for its defensive armament, plus a remotely-controlled HL 131 Z tail gun position.

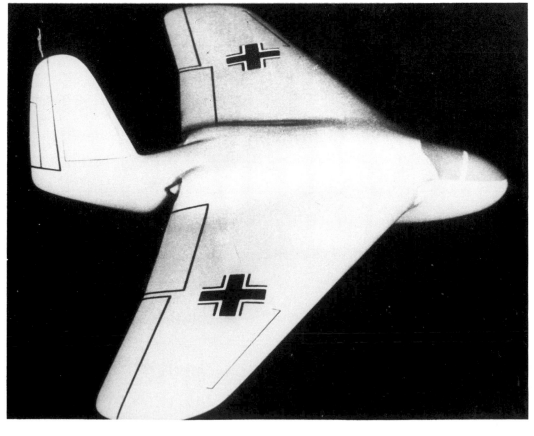

Left: The delta-winged Li L 10 remained a design project only. A few models and a mock-up of the aircraft were produced in 1943/44.

Horten Ho (Go) 229

The Horten Ho 229, which was also designated Gotha Go 229 at the beginning of 1945, was not intended solely as a flying-wing fighter, but mainly as a fighter-bomber. Viewing of the Ho 229 model took place on 7 September 1944, and on 23 November there was an evaluation of the design by General Engineer Herrman (OKL F1-E), as a result of which the mid-wing section was redesigned. The Gotha P 60 project then underwent a lengthy comparative evaluation, which delayed the development and building of the first machine.

The second, powered by two jet engines, was flown on 2 February 1945 by Erwin Ziller at Oranienburg. The third aircraft was in an advanced state of completion by the end of the war. As a fighter-bomber, the Go 229 A-1 was intended to take all current bomb types, but the approaching end of the war prevented its development.

Below: The tailless Go 229 was intended as a fighter-bomber – an intermediate stage between heavy fighter and high-speed bomber. The photograph shows the V 2 at Oranienburg.

Arado Ar 234

Increasing performance requirements led the RLM to announce a project for the construction of a jet-powered reconnaissance aircraft of 2,200km range. In the late autumn of 1940 Arado began preliminary design work under Director Walter Blume. By the beginning of 1941 the project design stage had been reached, and the E 370 design was produced in October 1941 and submitted to the Technische Amt.

From this finally came the Ar 234, a single-seat aircraft with an unswept shoulder-mounted wing, an all-round-vision cockpit, two jet engines and a single fin and rudder. Arado initially avoided the problems of a retractable undercarriage. Landings were to be made on an underfuselage skid and two outrigger skids under the engines, and take-off was from a disposable trolley, with rocket assistance.

In April 1942 Arado received the order from Generalfeldmarshall Milch to build six test aircraft, and this was increased to twenty on 20 December 1942. On 19 February 1943 it was decided to build two aircraft with retractable undercarriages, to be used for tests for a high-speed bomber. At the beginning of June that same year, a further order for twenty aircraft with retractable undercarriages was issued.

Since the development of the first Jumo 004 jet engines was taking longer than expected, tests of the Ar 234 V 1 were severely delayed. In mid-July 1943 the first prototype was disassembled and sent for testing to Rheine, where it was reassembled and fitted

Left: A mock-up of the Ar 234 B-2 cockpit, used for training on the Ar 234 series of Blitzbombers.

Right: Another shot of the B-2 cockpit mock-up, showing clearly the engine controls on the pilot's left.

with two Jumo 004s. Its first flight took place on 30 July 1943, with Flugkapitän Selle at the controls. At the end of August the V 1 was badly damaged on landing after three test flights. The Ar 234 V 2 became available from 13 September.

At the end of September the third machine was taken to Alt-Lönnewitz, where it underwent tests for the planned pressurised-cabin, tandem-seat version with a landing skid, the Ar 234 A. Meanwhile, the RLM issued an order that all aircraft had to have undercarriages, and consequently the A series were not built.

The ninth prototype had at first a retractable nosewheel, and was thus the test model for the B series, production of which began at Alt-Lönnewitz at the end of 1943. The first flight of the V 9 took place on 12 March 1944, and the first zero-series aircraft became available in June 1944. A short while later a small series of Ar 234 B-1 reconnaissance aircraft were built; these had the PATIN 11/12 three-axis navigation system, a built-in movie camera system and two 300lit drop tanks.

The Ar 234 B-2 could carry a total of three 500kg bombs under the fuselage and engine nacelles, or a single PC 1400 anti-armour bomb as an alternative. With a flying weight of approximately 8,000kg the aircraft had a maximum speed of 700km/h. On 2 October 1944 the order was issued for the Ar 234

B-2 to be used as a bomber. Up to 14 December 1944 116 Ar 234s were built, of which some 55 were delivered to KG 76.

Up to February 1945 all 210 aircraft of the B-series were delivered, and production was stopped in favour of the four-jet C-series, which was to be built at Alt-Lönnewitz and Brandenburg-Neuendorf. It was hoped that a monthly production rate of 500 aircraft would be reached by November 1945. For the Ar 234 C-series, the V 6 prototype with four separate engines was the first available, followed by the V 8. From the summer of 1944 the Ar 234 V 13 with paired jet engines and retractable undercarriage became available. At the end of September and October 1944 respectively, the V 19 to V 21 models followed. The V 21 model, tested at Küpper-Sagen (Niederschlesien), was the forerunner of the C-series and made its first flight on 16 October 1944.

The C-1 reconnaissance aircraft was followed by the C-2, a high-speed bomber with no defensive armament and a maximum bomb load of 1,500kg. The C-3 was a multi-role bomber intended for high-speed bombing, night-fighter and fighter-bomber applications. Its armament consisted of two fixed MG 151/20 machine guns in the nose and tail. The C-5 high-speed bomber was initially intended to have a two-man cockpit, and the RLM viewed the first mock-up on 30 October 1944.

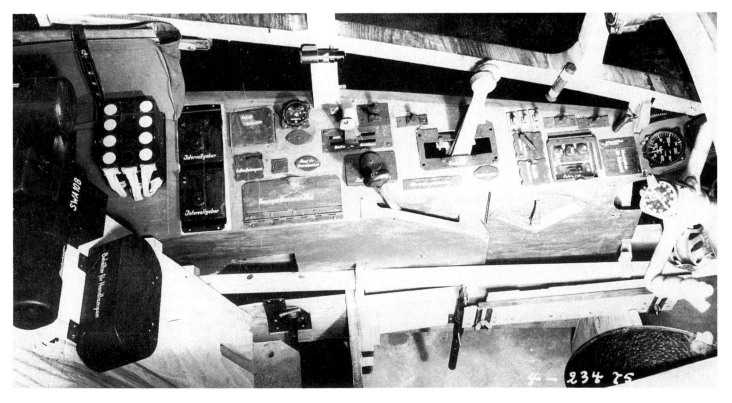

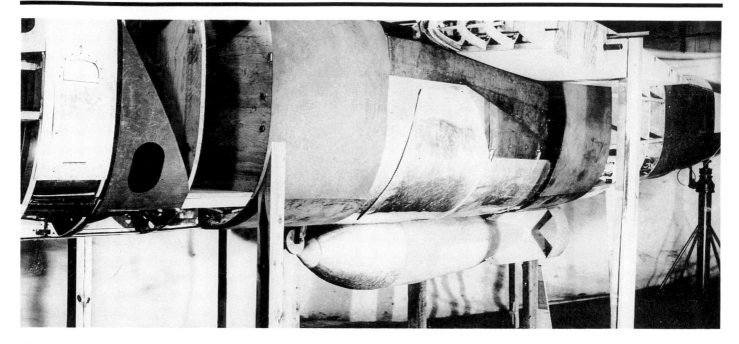

Above: This full-scale model of the Ar 234 fuselage was used for various loading trials with wooden model bombs.

Below: The Ar 234 V 9 (Works No.130009) flew for the first time on 12 March 1944 and was used for bomb-dropping trials.

Opposite page, top: After tests with Einsatzkommando Lukesch, the Ar 234 B-2 was attached to III./KG 76, which from 6 December 1944 was commanded by Major Hans-Georg Bätcher.

Opposite page, bottom: Arado Ar 234 B-2 F1+BT, with D. Lukesch at the controls, heads for take-off on 12 January 1944.

Because of the approaching end of the war, however, this aircraft was never built. Two Jumo 004D engines were planned for the Ar 234 C-8, the last bomber design. Only two MG 151/20 machine guns were installed as forward armament.

Production of the Ar 234 C-3 and C-5 versions was intended to be a main series. By the end of the war, however, only a few Ar 234 C-1 production aircraft and some C-3 pre-series aircraft had been assembled, and only a few of these had their engines installed. For the C-3 series the test aircraft V 21 to V 25 were used, while V 28 was used for the C-5 series. The V 29 to V 40 models were never built. Three C-3 series aircraft had been built by February 1945. However, as a result of a change from B4 to J2 fuel, their delivery was considerably delayed. The first aircraft with BZA 1B equipment was intended to be delivered to KG 76 in the summer of 1945. A few Ar 234s were tested in April 1945 by Hauptmann Lukesch.

Geheim! T4-23453

Opposite page, top: This Ar 234 B-2 (F1+MT, Works No.140173) was the first Arado jet bomber captured almost undamaged.

Opposite page, bottom: The two-seat Ar 234 C-5 ultra-high-speed bomber was to replace the B-2 in the summer of 1945. However, the war ended before it was finished. The mock-up is seen here.

Above: The test model for the C-3 series was the V 13 (Works No.130023), flight-tested on 6 September 1944.

Right: The Ar 234 V 20 was destroyed in an Allied air raid on Wesendorf on 4 April 1944.

High-Altitude Bombers

Right: The pressurised cabin for a Ju 49a. On 1 November 1935 the prototype reached an altitude of 12,500m.

Below: From 20 March 1940 the Hs 128 V 2 (D-ARHD) was used as a high-altitude research aircraft by the Deutschen Versuchsanstalt für Luftfahrt (DVL - German Aeronautical Research Institute).

Junkers Ju 49, EF61 and Ju 86 P/R

Development of the Ju 86 long-range high-altitude reconnaissance and bomber aircraft drew on experience with the Ju 49 of as long ago as 1931, and with the pressure-cabin equipped Ju EF 61.

Construction of the Ju 49 ba high-altitude research aircraft began at the end of 1929, and on 2 October 1931 the first flight of the one aircraft built (D-2688, Works No.3701) took place. By 1935 altitudes of 13,000m had been reached. The aircraft flew from the DLV at Adlershof.

Two Ju EF 61s were built, the E 1 (Works No.4931) and E-2 (Works No.4932), which first flew on 4 March and 18 December 1937 respectively. The E-1 crashed on 19 September 1937 from 3,500m altitude. Like the first aircraft, the second also had two DB 600 engines, but had only one fixed MG 15 as defensive armament. This aircraft crashed shortly after its first flight and was completely destroyed.

The following design, the Ju 86 P, was fitted with the Jumo 207 heavy-oil engine, a development of the Jumo 205. In September

Below: The two-seat Ju 49a was used for initial testing of high-altitude aircraft. The order for this machine was placed on 24 October 1929.

Above: Only two Ju EF 61s (E1 and E2) were produced. The E1 (Works No.4931) first flew on 4 March 1937.

Below: The E1 was completely destroyed in a crash from a height of 3,500m on 19 September 1937.

Above: The cabin of the EF 61 E1, showing insulation against the cold.

Left: Seven zero-series Ju EF 61s were planned for the building programme of 1936, to test the type's suitability as a high-altitude bomber with 5,000km range.

Opposite page, top: Flight-testing of the Ju EF 61 E2 (Works No.4932) began on 18 December 1937.

Opposite page, bottom: The Ju 86 P-1 was at first unarmed when it was attached to 1./Reconnaissance Group ObdL, where it reached speeds of about 390km/h at altitudes of 12,000m.

1939 the RLM issued the order to build 40 high-altitude aircraft in long-distance reconnaissance and heavy-bomber versions. Component production began in November 1939. From the Ju 86 D-1/D-2 series arose the Ju 86 H, which later materialised as the Ju 86 P.

From February 1940 the Ju 86 PV 1 was tested at Dessau, followed in March by PV 2 and PV 3, with two-seat high-altitude cabins and two 907hp (667kW) Jumo 207 A engines. The PV 3 had greater wing span (25.6m), and served as the first pre-series aircraft of the Ju 86 P-1 series. Up to August 1940, 43 test flights above 10,000m, with a total duration of 40 flying hours, had taken place. The first high-altitude night-flight of a Ju 86 P took place as part of this programme.

In the same year, mass-production of the P-1 high-altitude bomber and P-2 reconnaissance aircraft began. Forty aircraft, mostly converted from the G-series, were delivered to reconnaissance group Ob.d.L. (2. and 4. Squadrons), 2.(F)/Aufkl.Gr.33 and the Kommando Rowehl. In addition to having increased wing area, this version differed in having an improved cabin which was provided with a pressure-sealed high-altitude chamber. Powered by the Jumo 207 A-1 engine, the Ju 86 P-2 reached an altitude of 12,500m at a flying weight of 9,500kg. At first these aircraft had no defensive armament. The P-1 high-altitude bomber could carry a maximum of four SC 250 bombs. It was only occasionally used on bombing missions, and its main application was long-distance reconnaissance.

After three Ju 86 Ps were shot down by Spitfire Vs with high-altitude engines, it became clear that increased flight performance was an absolute necessity. Development of the Ju 86 R-1 and R-2 versions with Jumo 207 B-3 engines with GM-1 (nitrous oxide) injection, which developed a power of 1,000hp (735kW), began, These engines, plus increased wing area, enabled the aircraft to climb to a maximum of 14,800m. However, as early as September 1942 the Spitfire IX was able to engage the Ju 86 R. A few aircraft were used for reconnaissance missions up to 1944 by Versuchsverband Ob.d.L. on the eastern and southern fronts.

Above: Engine testing on a Ju 86 P-1 at Dessau. The usual power-plant for this aircraft was two Jumo 207 A-1 engines.

Opposite page, top: The Ju 86 R-1 was the successor to the P-1. It could fly at 420km/h at 9,000m, and had an endurance of 60min at 13,700m.

Opposite page, bottom: The Ju 86 RV 29 takes off. It was powered by two Jumo 207 B-3 engines and was used to test new variants.

High-Altitude Supercharger Development

The poor performance of the only German high-altitude bomber to be mass produced, the Ju 86 P/R, meant that it could no longer be used over western Europe. Furthermore, tests on the Do 215, Do 217, He 111, and Ju 88 with turbochargers did not get beyond the prototype stage. Only one Do 215 B-6 equipped with the TK-9A turbocharger was available to the DVL. The Do 217 V 13 (DB+BC, Works No.0032) also had the TK-9 turbocharger. The V 14 (Works No.0030) was fitted with a BMW 801 A-1 engine, or alternatively the DB 603 with the TK-11 turbocharger. This was used as a test aircraft for the Do 217 M-8 series. The Do 217 M-1/U1 was a Do 217 M with the Do 217 C fuselage mid-section and 68m² wing area. It was powered by two DB 603 high-altitude engines with

TK-9 turbochargers. The replacement of these by Jumo 211/213 engines with TK-9 and TK-11 turbochargers was planned, as was use of the DB 603 U. The 'Braunschweig' test model conversion was an He 111 H-6 with two DB 601 E engines with TK-9AC turbochargers. Its estimated ceiling was 11,000m at 10,000kg flying weight. From 1943 further development with a pressurised cockpit and TK-15 turbochargers took place. An He 111 (Works No.7880) was tested with Jumo 211 F engines and two 9-2281 turbochargers, but suffered from very high engine temperatures. The cost of this equipment militated against further developments. The necessary improvements in performance were therefore sought from engines of higher power such as the DB 610, BMW 801 TJ or Jumo 211 E/F series.

Below: A model of a high-altitude engine layout, consisting of a DB 601 A fitted with a TK 9A turbocharger.

Right: Using a new engine configuration, the Do 215 B-6 was able to reach 580km/h at an altitude of 9,000m.

Right: The 'Braunschweig' conversion was carried out by Dornier at Friedrichshafen. The exhausts of the turbochargers for the DB engines are over the upper surface of the wing.

Right: The 'Posen' conversion consisted of equipping an He 111 H-6 with a TK 9 AC turbocharger. This development led to the high-altitude bomber version, the He 111 R.

Dornier Do 217 P

In September 1941 the design of the P 183 and Do 217 began, and eventually led to the Do 217 P high-altitude bomber. In place of the highly sophisticated engines, Dornier, like Henschel, settled for a conventional engine layout consisting of two DB 603 S-0 engines and one DB 605 T as power for the central compressor which provided the two DB 603s with pre-cooled, pre-pressurised inlet air. The first static tests of these centrally supercharged (HZ) engines began at Stuttgart in October 1941. From 1942 the fuselage of a Do 217 E-2 was used for a variety of engine tests. A converted aircraft of the same type with increased wing area (67m²) was used for vibration and load tests for the proposed Do 217 P series.

From the Do 217 E-2 (BK+IR, Works No.1229), came the first of the initial three test aircraft of the high-altitude Do 217 P. On 6 June 1942 the Do 217 PV 1 made its first flight. In mid-August, after a few test flights reaching an altitude of 11,300m, Dornier fitted wings of increased area. By 2 April 1943 23 test flights totalling 34 flying hours had taken place, an altitude of 13,000m having been exceeded on three occasions. The maximum

Left: The Do 217 PV 1 (Works No.1229, BK+IR) first flew on 6 June 1942, and reached a maximum altitude of 13,400m.

Above: At least four further Do 217 test aircraft were produced apart from the PV 1. The PV5 and PV6 were scrapped in March 1944.

altitude reached was 13,650m. From the end of August, flights were carried out using the central supercharger. Up to this time tests had been severely disrupted because of strong vibrations in the turbocharger and problems with the propellers. In the meantime, the RLM decided to build a further three test aircraft, because testing of the Hs 130 had been subject to severe delays. After various flights with Daimler-Benz engines, which gave only a small increase in high-altitude performance, the Do 217 PV 1 went to Friedrichshafen in April to have its wing area increased to 71.0m². The Do 217 PV 2 with the earlier air-coolers became available with Daimler-Benz engines from September 1942. In March 1943 comparative test flights took place, using the PV 2 with the old cooler and PV 3 with the new one.

The Do 217 PV 2 was lost as a result of an air raid at Cazaux, where it had been sent for bombing trials. The Do 217 PV 4 reached a maximum altitude of 15,200m, where it could still climb at 0.25m/s, before the test was ended when stability became too great a problem. The Do 217 PV 5 and PV 6 were respectively 95 and 80 per cent complete by 1943, but were scrapped on 11 March 1944. By the end of 1943 the whole high-altitude programme, including turbocharger development, was discontinued because of the war situation. Work on central turbocharging was stopped in 1944 in favour of the DB 627 design. The PV 1 and PV 2 were lost owing to enemy action, together with an Hs 130 E-0, on 5 September 1944.

Henschel Hs 130

The Henschel Hs 128 V 1 (D-APXB) and V 2 (D-ARHD) high-altitude research aircraft, which made their first flights on 11 April 1939 and 20 February 1940 respectively, were the forerunners of the Hs 130 high-altitude bomber and reconnaissance aircraft.

The first two prototypes (Hs 130 AV 1 GH+OM and AV 2 GH+ON) flew for the first time on 23 May and 17 July 1940 respectively. Between August 1940 and January 1941 seven zero-series (A-0) aircraft followed, most of which were powered by DB 601 A or DB 601 R-0 high-altitude engines. Then, in 1941, there followed the first research aircraft for testing the Jumo 208. Some aircraft (Works Nos.3003, and 3005 to 3008) were also tested with the GM-1 injection system, Works No.3005 being fitted with DB 605 C aircraft engines. These aircraft were destroyed in an Allied air raid on Echterdingen on 5 September 1944.

After the next series, the B-0, was cancelled during the design stage, three Hs C-0s

were produced. The first prototype, the Hs 130 C-0/V 3 (Works No.0011, NK+EA) made its first flight on 10 November 1941 and was, like the V 4, powered by two BMW 801 MA-2 engines.

The third C-0 (NK+EC) was fitted with DB 603 A-0 engines, and was abandoned by Henschel in May 1944. The planned high-altitude aircraft (up to Works No.0030) were dropped in favour of the Hs 130 E, and the D-0 series was likewise cancelled by the RLM. The E-0 series had a centralised supercharging system in the fuselage centre section, which provided both DB 603 high-altitude engines with pre-compressed air. The fuselage was taken from the A-0 series, and the wings from the C-0. Of the five zero-series aircraft (Works Nos.0051 to 0055), two crashed (in December 1942 and September 1943), a third was destroyed in an air raid on Daimler-Benz on 5 September 1944, and another (Works No.0055) was mothballed. Together with at least three HS

Left: The majority of Hs 130 A-0s built were powered by two DB 601 R-0 engines fitted with the GM-1 nitrous oxide injection system. Testing began in August 1940.

130 E-1 (Works Nos.130040, 130060 and 130070), the remaining E-0 aircraft were used for high-altitude research until the summer of 1944.

However, the third E-1 model soon showed that the aircraft was not ready for mass production. All designs, notably that with a PC 1400X for altitudes of up to 14,000m, were dropped, as no suitable guidance equipment was available.

Retrofitting of defensive armament to the HS 130 E-1 took place as quickly as possible, using two remotely-controlled barbettes which had already been subjected to extensive wind-tunnel testing. In the summer of 1944 the last operational Hs 130 was mothballed at Schöne-feld, and its further history is unknown.

Right: An oblique view of the Hs 130 A-0 from the specification of August 1940, which applied to Works Nos.131 3003 to 3010.

Right: A wind tunnel model of the Hs 130 C-0, of which only three (C-0/V 3 to V 5, Works Nos.131 0011 to 0013) were eventually produced.

Right: Only a few Hs 130 E-0s were produced, and most were used for factory testing either by the manufacturer or by Daimler Benz at Echterdingen.

Heinkel He 177
H/He 274

Shortly before the outbreak of the Second World War, Heinkel was involved with the design of a high-altitude version of the He 177 A. It was to operate at 15,000m and to have a range of 3,000km with a maximum bomb load of 2,000kg. In October 1941 the RLM ordered the building of six test examples of the He 177 H, which used the fuselage and cabin of the He 177 A-1 but was to be powered by four turbocharged DB 605 engines, and to have twin fins and rudders. The RLM required that part of the construction work should be done by a French firm to relieve pressure on the Heinkel works.

The development order, which came slightly later, designated the aircraft 'high-altitude bomber He 274', and divided construction between Heinkel (Marienehe) and Farman (Suresnes, Paris). Armament was to be an MG 131 in the lower cockpit region, and single MG 131 Zs in the dorsal and ventral positions. A remotely-controlled rotatable turret was also tested on an He 177 A. The take-off weight had to be less than 29,500kg if the high-altitude performance was not to be adversely affected.

Problems with hydraulics and wing-stiffness, as well as uncertainties over the power-plant, delayed delivery, which had been

Below: Heinkel He 177 B-5 prototype V 101, Works No.535550, which made its first flight on 20 December 1943.

Above: The pressurised cabin of the He 274 V 1 was based on that designed for the He 177 A-4.
Below: A full-scale model of the planned mass-production fin and rudder for the He 274 in the wind tunnel at Meudon.

planned for the end of July 1943. Components for the He 274 V 1 were manufactured in France, but Heinkel carried out the assembly. Delivery of the first pre-series aircraft was still awaited as late as September 1944.

The zero-series had already been cancelled by the RLM on 20 April 1944. Only the He 274 V 1 to V 3 and an incomplete airframe remained for test use. Furthermore, the planned 'safety cockpit with ejector seats' had to be abandoned because development had become too costly. The He 277, the mass-production version of the He 177 with four single BMW 801 engines, based on the He 274, had to be dropped owing to the non-availability of constructional materials.

The He 274 V 1 was eventually assembled at the beginning of July 1944, when Allied troops were about to capture the Farman works. It was impossible to transfer the aircraft to Germany, and an attempt was made to destroy it by blowing up the engines. However, this failed, and the aircraft remained undamaged.

The second machine was not ready for flight testing. At the end of the war the Farman factory was renamed Atéliers Aéronautiques de Suresnes (AAS), and the prototypes were therefore designated AAS 01 and 02. On 27 December 1945 AAS 01, ex He 274 V 1, made its first flight, and from 1948 it was used to fly scale models of the French SO 400 research aircraft. The second He 274, powered by captured DC 603 A engines with four TK-11 turbochargers, served as a flying test bed until it was scrapped in 1953.

Above: The He 274 V 1 was redesignated AAS 01 and repaired after the end of the war, despite damage which occurred shortly before the German retreat.

Junkers Ju 388

The modified airframe of the Ju 188, with a new, low-drag fuselage (the ventral turret was removed) and a tail-gun position, was designated Ju 388. In 1943 the war situation in the west demanded a new bomber with better high-altitude performance. In September of that year the transformation of the Ju 188 into the Ju 388, using the BMW 801 J-1, began in earnest as part of the 'Hubertus' programme. This included development of the high-altitude night and all-weather fighter versions Ju 388 J (at least two of which were flight-tested from 1944), as well as of the Ju 388 L high-altitude reconnaissance version, which was produced in small numbers in the autumn of 1944. Its range was 3,400km, and

service ceiling 13,500m. However, with a maximum speed of 615km/h at 12,500m, this aircraft was slower than the Ju 188 T-1.

At least four aircraft of the zero-series (K-0, Works Nos.230151 et seq), were known to be at Dessau, Prague, and Rechlin. However, development was abandoned in favour of the Ju 388 L-1. The first prototype of the K-series was the Ju 388 V 3 (PE+IC, Works No.500003). This aircraft was located at Merseburg in April 1944 and at Rechlin in January 1945. The Ju 388 V 4 (PE+ID, Works No.500004), the second prototype, was at Dessau on 22 February 1945, but no fuel was available for it.

Right: The pressurised cabins of the Ju 388 L-1 and K-1 were virtually identical. The V 3 and V 4 aircraft were used for high-altitude bomber development.

Above: This Ju 388 crashed on a long-range flight near Lechfeld, in the late summer of 1944.

Left: The Ju 388 was basically equipped with one FHL 131 Z in a tail barbette, the FA 15 remote control system, and a PVE 11 gunsight.

Top right: The blind-flying panel of the Ju 388 L-1 (Works No.500006), which was similar to the equipment in the Ju 388 K-1.

Right: This BMW 801 TJ-0 caught fire on an overland flight, necessitating an emergency landing in open country.

Left: The cabin hatch of the Ju 388 J-1, K-1, and L-1.

Left: In April 1945 this Ju 388 was captured on a German airfield.

Long-Range Bombers

Above: A drawing of a Do 19 from the official tender of the Dornier Works to the Technische Amt of the RLM.

Below: A drawing of a production Ju 89 A-1 with four gun positions.

Dornier Do 19

Despite the recommendation of General-leutnant Walter Wever, both the Do 19 and Ju 89 long-range bombers were cancelled in 1937 after his death. Instead, experience with the Ju 87 in Spain led to the idea of developing a long-range dive-bomber (Bomber A). The Heinkel He 177A was therefore originally built as a dive-bomber, but owing to its inadequate strength could only be used for level bombing. In 1943 the concept of a four-engined long-range bomber was again given priority for a short while. All efforts towards building a new long-range bomber on the lines of the Ju 89 and the Do 19 had been abandoned by that time because of the state of the war.

General Wever had foreseen the need for a similar but lower-powered aircraft as early as 1934. The four-engined strategic long-range bomber had to carry its bomb load of four SC 250s over 2,000km. The flying weight amounted to 19,000kg, and its defensive armament consisted of manually-operated turrets with MG 15s above and below the fuselage, although 20mm guns were also envisaged. An unarmed Do 19 V 1 made its first flight on 26 October 1936.

In April 1937 all work on the so-called 'Ural Bomber' was stopped, and the Do 19 V 2 and V 3 prototypes were scrapped before they flew. The Do 19 V 1 was presumably used as a transport aircraft up to 1938.

Left: A Do 19 V 1 heavy bomber, armed with at least two MG 15s and two heavy machine guns.

Left: The V 1 and V 2 versions of the four-engined Do 19 were to be powered by Bramo 322 H and 132 F engines respectively. The V 1 flew for the first time on 28 October 1936.

Junkers Ju 89

Like the Do 19, the Ju 89 arose from the long-range bomber proposal of 1934. The performance, bomb load, and armament was very similar to that of the Do 19, although the flying weight exceeded 22,800kg. The first prototype (D-AFIT, Works No.4911) made its first flight on 11 April 1934, powered by Jumo 210A engines 680hp (500kW), and the V 2 aircraft followed in the spring of 1937, powered by four 960hp (705kW) DB 600A engines. From the V 3 Junkers developed the large Ju 90 commercial airliner. In the summer of 1938, components of the Ju 89 V 3 were incorporated in the Ju 90 V 4 (D-ADLH, Works No.4910), which was the prototype for the Ju 90 transport aircraft.

With the progress of long-range-bomber development, the Ju 89 V 1 and V 2 models were presumably scrapped, so that parts were not available for the Ju 90.

Below: The Ju 89 V 1 (Works No.4911, D-AFIT) on the hard-standing at Dessau.

Above: The cockpit of the Ju 89 V 1 (Works No.4911, D-AFIT). The pilot and co-pilot were seated in tandem. On the right, the gun mounting was still to be fitted with an MG 15.

Below: The heavy ventral gun mounting of the Ju 89, intended for 20mm cannon.

Focke-Wulf Fw 200

The Fw 200 V 2 (D-AETA) was converted to an auxiliary long-range reconnaissance aircraft by the Rechlin Experimental Establishment in the summer of 1939. Shortly afterwards, the Fw 200 V 3 (D-AMHC) and V 4 followed. The latter, like the Fw 200 V 10, was fitted with two movie cameras, but on 23 November 1939 it crashed at the beginning of its first long-range flight at Jever.

At this time the possibility was being investigated of using the aircraft for attacks against shipping, using a variety of different armaments. The RLM accepted the similarly equipped Fw 200 C, and in September 1939 ordered a pre-series batch of ten Fw 200 Cs. Up to the summer of 1940 the C-1 series was produced with bomb racks and single MG 15s in the two dorsal positions and the ventral posi-

tion. Additionally, it was planned to incorporate a ventral turret with one MG FF cannon firing forwards and downwards. Four SC 250 bombs could be carried on bomb racks located under the outer engine nacelles and inner wings, and 250kg bombs could also be carried in a bomb bay when the ventral gun position was removed. With additional fuel tanks, range was 5,000km at a cruising speed of 290km/h. Maximum speed was 355km/h at 5,000m altitude, and the service ceiling was 6,000m. The flying weight was 20,500kg, a figure which was on the outer limits of structural strength for auxiliary bombers. The powerplant comprised four BMW 132 H-1 radial engines of 999hp (735kW).

In addition to attacking Allied shipping (from 1 August 1940 to 9 February 1941 a total

Below: The Fw 200 C-1 (Works No.0013) could carry up to four heavy bombs under the outer wings as well as a load in the bomb bay.

of 85 vessels of 360,000 gross tons had been sunk, including the troop transport *Empress of Britain* on 26 October 1940), the Fw 200 C-1 also undertook reconnaissance for U-boats. In joint actions between the Luftwaffe and the German Navy, favourable results were obtained in the early years of the War. However, the limited number of operational Fw 200s did not allow widespread use.

With the introduction of the Fw 200 C-3 (from Works No.0070) in the summer of 1941, a structurally improved version was available with the more powerful BMW-Bramo 323 R-2 radial engine 1,200hp (883kW). The gun positions and the cockpit were now partially armoured. An MG FF cannon was fitted in the nose of the ventral gondola, and the forward dorsal gun position was constructed as a cupola. The external bomb racks could only carry two SD 1400, PC 1700, or SC 1800 bombs. The C-3/U4 version had a higher fuel capacity and could carry two LT S5 aerial torpedoes on the external bomb racks. This was tested by 4./KG 40 (which was also using the

Do 217) from 20 September 1941 to 31 May 1942. The MG 131 replaced the MG 15 in the rear dorsal position, and the forward ventral position was now fitted with an MG 151/20. Usually, the crew consisted of seven men.

In early 1941 the first seven aircraft using the 'Rostock' ship-search radar became available. Shortly afterwards this was replaced by the FuG 200 'Hohentwiel'. The Fw 200 C-4 series in particular had this equipment. In addition, the defensive armament was strengthened through the replacement of the HDL 151 in the forward dorsal turret by an MG 131 or MG 151/20, as had already taken place in the C-3/U1.

The Fw 200 C-5 was also used as a platform for two Hs 293 A-1 glide bombs. In addition, the defensive armament was strengthened by the introduction of MG 131s in the dorsal and rear ventral positions. The aircraft Works No.0114 was used as a weapons test bed at Tarnewitz. The improved C-6 series had an FuG 203 B radio-control system for the glide bombs, as well as an FuG 200 search radar.

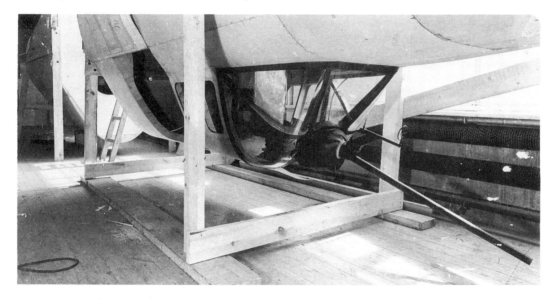

Left: The mock-up of the forward armament position, which was intended to carry MG 151/20 cannon for attacking shipping or ground targets.

Left: Production of the Fw 200 C-3/U2 at the beginning of 1941. In the foreground, Works No.0055 (DE+OJ) has its bomb doors open.

The planned C-8 long-range bomber was essentially a C-4 with an improved ventral turret, to provide better visibility for control of the Hs 293 guided weapons. The Kehl missile control system was tested by Erprobungskommando Garz in mid-November 1943 on Works No.0236 (C-8). However, in total, only eighteen Fw 200 C-8 glide-bomb carriers were produced. The majority of these aircraft later served as communications or long-range reconnaissance aircraft.

Up to February 1944 Focke-Wulf delivered over 260 reconnaissance and auxiliary bomber versions of the Fw 200 C.

Right: The Fw 200 C-3 was powered by four Bramo 323 R2 engines, and could carry a 5,400kg bomb load.

Below: A close-up of two of the four bombs carried externally by the Fw 200 C. Although its maximum load was intended to be SC 1800 bombs, it was more usually loaded with SC 250, SC 500, or PC 500.

Left: The Fw 200 C-5 had an L 151/1 with an HD 151 rotary mounting in both the dorsal and ventral forward positions.

Left: This Ju 290 A-5 (9V+BH) was fitted with an FuG 101 precision radar altimeter as well as FuG 200 ship-search radar.

Junkers Ju 290

Junkers developed the more powerful Ju 290 from the Ju 90 four-engined passenger and transport aircraft. In fact, the first four Ju 290s were converted Ju 90 B-1 transports, but they were soon followed by the Ju 290 A-1 series (Works Nos.0151-1059). The first test aircraft made its maiden flight on 16 July 1942, and on the basis of this transport aircraft the Ju 290 A-3 reconnaissance version with more powerful BMW 801 engines was developed and attached to long-range reconnaissance group (FAG) 5 from 1943. Maximum flight duration was 18 hours.

At least one of the five long-range reconnaissance aircraft of the A-4 series was used for glide-bomb testing with the Hs 293 and Fritz X controlled by the Kehl radio-control system. The A-5 series, which followed at the end of 1943, had two ETC 200 bomb racks and an additional nose-mounted MG 151/20. Eleven A-5s were produced.

At the beginning of 1944, tests of the Ju 290 A-7 began. This aircraft had a stronger airframe, the glazed nose of the A-4 as standard, seven MG 151/20s and one MG 131, and movie cameras for sideways photography. A capability for carrying guided bombs was also planned. The maximum speed of this version with BMW 801 Ds was 438km/h at 5,000m altitude, and factory data gives the range as 5,800km. Fourteen aircraft of the A-7 series were built at the Junkers works.

A single Ju 90 A-8 (Works No.0212) was planned as a special bomber, but although it was at Prague-Rusin in May 1945, it could not be produced. The Ju 290 A-9 had two hydraulically-operated turrets with four MG 151/20 machine guns and an improved tail-gun position with two MG 151/20s to strengthen the defensive armament. Its maximum bomb load was 3,000kg, and flight characteristics were more or less similar to those of the A-7. About

Right: A rare shot of two Ju 290 of 1./FAG 5 over the North Atlantic.

fifty Ju 290s were manufactured up to the end of production in the summer of 1944.

The Ju 290 B-1 series was intended to be mass produced with an additional four-gun position at both nose and tail. Construction of the Ju 290 B-1 began in September 1943, but experience with FAG 5 showed that the defensive armament was inadequate. The prototype of the B-1 was inspected on 16 October 1943, but the remote-controlled gun positions did not gain the approval of either the RLM or Erprobungskommando Garz. Work on the Ju 290 B was eventually stopped on 30 June 1944.

Below: This Ju 290 A-7 (KR+LL) of 2./FAG 5, which crash-landed on 1 April 1944, was only slightly damaged and could be repaired.

Messerschmitt Me 264

As a predecessor to a strategic bomber, Messerschmitt developed the Me 264 under the supervision of Dr Konrad. On 23 December 1942 this shoulder-wing aircraft, the first German four-engined aircraft to have a tricycle undercarriage, made its first flight, powered by four Jumo 211 J engines. Unfortunately this lasted only 22 minutes because a fault prevented retraction of the undercarriage. On 23 March 1943 the V 1 suffered an undercarriage failure. Between August 1943 and April 1944 the Me 264 V 1 (RE+EN) was fitted with four BMW 801 G-2 radial engines. The second prototype was also intended to have BMW engines, and had its wingspan increased to 43m. The unarmed V 2 was lost during an air raid in 1944. On 16 April 1944 the V 1 was transferred to Memmingen, where it was lost four days later in an air raid.

During testing the powerplant was modified several times, and the test programme was delayed by stability problems and tail flutter.

The prototype for the planned A series, the Me 264 V 3, was not built. It had been hoped that this aircraft, again with 43m wingspan, would attain 565km/h at a height of 8,000m at a flying weight of 49,000kg. Maximum range was thought to be 12,500km. With the A series, flying weight had increased to 56,000kg and range to 15,000km.

The planned 'America Bomber', the Me 264 B, was designed with six engines. It remained a design only, however, because the war situation, and especially the shortage of raw materials, meant that mass production of such large aircraft was no longer possible.

Above: The still incomplete cockpit of the Me 264 V 1.

Opposite page, bottom: The Me 264 V 1 (Works No.264 00001, RE+EN) was tested in June 1943. It had Jumo 211 J in-line engines driving VS 11 propellers.

Right: After a crash-landing, the Me 264 V 1 was fitted with four BMW 801 MG-2 engines. Altogether, this machine made 49 flights.

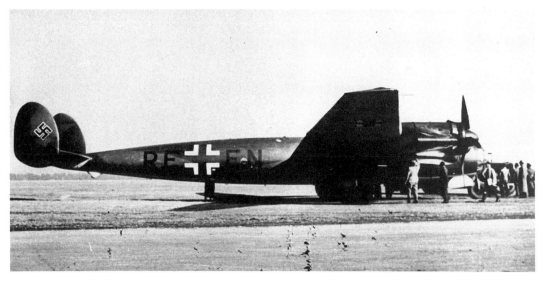

Junkers Ju 390

The six-engined Ju 390 was developed by Dipl-Ing Kraft from the Ju 290. Construction of the prototype began in March 1943, and on 20 October 1943 the Ju 390 V 1 (GH+UK), a conversion of the Ju 90 V 6, flew for the first time at Merseburg with Flight Staff Engineer Bader at the controls. Further flight testing at Prague up to December 1943 gave encouraging results.

The Ju 390 had a Ju 290 fuselage lengthened to 34.2m and wingspan of 50.6m. An additional undercarriage leg was located beneath the central engine on each wing. Payload was 10,000kg, with a range of 8,000km at 330km/h at 2,000m altitude.

In April 1944 a production plan was prepared for the Ju 390s V 2 to V 7 plus twenty series aircraft. In June of that year, however, the series was cancelled, with only the test aircraft programme remaining. In fact, only the Ju 390 V 2 (RC+DA), was built. This was transferred to Rechlin-Lärz on 3 February 1945 and presumably scrapped.

Below: The first prototype of the Ju 390, tested on 20 October 1943 by Junkers at Prague.

Focke-Wulf Ta 400

A competitive design for the strategic bomber was the Focke-Wulf Ta 400, of which only a wind tunnel model exists. This long-range multi-purpose aircraft with a nine-man crew was the subject of a Focke-Wulf design document in October 1943. It was to have six BMW 801 E radial engines and a flying weight of 62,500kg. Wingspan was 42m, and overall length 29.4m. A maximum bomb load of 10,000kg could be carried in the 9m-long bomb bay, as well as an external load of Hs 293 and Hs 294 glide bombs. Defensive armament consisted of one FDL 103Z and two MK 103 cannon in the nose, HDL 151Z barbettes in the front and rear dorsal positions, an HL 131 V in a tail barbette, and an FDL 151Z in a ventral barbette. The fuel capacity of 27,000lit gave a range of over 9,000km. Focke-Wulf envisaged the Ta 400 primarily as an anti-ship aircraft, or for long-range maritime reconnaissance and the engagement over the Atlantic of enemy aircraft which were attacking German U-boats. As with the Me 264 B, the design was abandoned in favour of the emergency fighter building programme of mid-1944.

Right: A wind tunnel model of the Ta 400. This projected long-range bomber was to have a wingspan of 42m and a flying weight of 62,500kg.

Right: Development of the Ta 400 was discontinued in the summer of 1944, when material for the production of such large aircraft was no longer available.

Junkers Ju 488

After powerplant and strength problems with the He 177, Junkers offered the Technische Amt an alternative solution at the beginning of 1944, in the form of the four-engined Ju 488. This design was based on the modular construction of the Ju 388, and used the complete forward fuselage section, pressurised cabin and wings of the Ju 388 K/L, the fuselage mid-section and tail of the Ju 188 E, the wooden ventral turret of the Ju 88 A-15/Ju 388 K and the tail of the Ju 288 C. Additional sections were used to extend the fuselage and wings. Manufacture of fuselage and the new wing mid-section was to take place at the former Latécoére Works at Toulouse. In July 1944, however, the French Resistance destroyed the fuselages of the Ju 488 V 401 and V 402, which were awaiting rail transport for final assembly at Bernburg.

Since the fuselage construction of the two prototypes (V 401 and V 402) was not satisfactory, a new wider and 3m longer welded steel-tube structure with aluminium plating for the forward and middle fuselage, and fabric covering in the tail region, was planned for the Ju 488 V 403 to 406, and the ventral turret was deleted. This method of construction was also planned for the A series, intended for mid-1945. In place of the four BMW 801 TJ engines of 1,.800hp (1,324kW) take-off power, Junkers intended the V 403 to be powered by four Jumo 222s 2,500hp (1,840kW). There was an undercarriage leg under each engine nacelle. In the fuselage mid-section V 403 had a remote-controlled barbette with two MG 151/20, and at the tail two MG 131. Maximum bomb load was increased from 2,000 to 5,000kg, and range increased from 2,000km to 3,400km at an average speed of 490km/h at 7,000m altitude.

In the late summer of 1944 the RLM stopped all work on the Ju 488. In January 1945 a licence to build the Ju 488 in Japan was granted, but none were produced.

Heinkel He 343

Under the project designation P 1068, Heinkel developed a four-engined jet bomber with various types of engine which was later given the designation 'He Strahlbomber 16t', and, even later, He 343. It was in effect a simple enlargement of the Ar 234. In order to proceed to mass production as quickly as possible, Heinkel scaled up the original aircraft by a factor of 1.5. The first power-plant was four Jumo 004C turbojets with a static thrust of 9.8kN. The airframe weighed 5,260kg, and was thus 1,810kg lighter than its competitor, the Ju 287. Maximum bomb load was expected to be 2,000kg, compared with the 3,000kg planned for the Ju 287, and with this load a range of 1,600km was anticipated. Overall, the performance of the He 343 was substantially similar to that of the Ju 287, but a fewer raw materials and only four engines were necessary.

In the summer of 1944 Heinkel received the order to build two prototypes (Works Nos.850061 and 850062). The previously planned 18 additional test aircraft were cancelled. The He 343 V 1 was intended for flight and engine testing. According to the construc-

tion specification of 15 April 1944, it had neither bomb racks nor double-glazing, but only one FuG 17 and the air supply equipment with cooler in the cockpit. The aircraft was later used for diving tests, with ejector seats for the test pilots.

The second prototype was used to test armament and radio equipment. It was to have a double-glazed cockpit, air supply equipment with cooler in the wing leading edge, and a simpler undercarriage with reduced track. At the same time, bomb-carrying gear was produced, with the intention of fitting it at a later stage. The production specification also provided for one further airframe.

Several wind tunnel models and two full-scale fuselage mock-ups, along with some components of the two prototypes, were produced up to September 1944. On 15 October 1944 the RLM decided that all tools and gauges for the He 343 should be destroyed. One month later, on 19 November 1944, it was ordered that all parts so far produced for the He 343 V 1 and V 2 should be put into storage, so that construction could be continued at a later date.

Right: A model of the He 343 jet bomber, which was never built, although parts for two prototypes were produced when the RLM initiated development.

Junkers Ju 287

The war diary of the Head of the TLR shows that, on 17 March 1945, the Ju 287 was regarded as a first stage in the development of the future turbojet heavy-bomber (TL-Grossbomber). In March 1944 the pre-specification for two prototypes (Ju 287 V 1 and V 2) was drawn up. Up to the summer of 1944 it was expected that over a hundred Ju 287s would be ordered. The specification quoted a normal bomb load of 3,000kg with a range of around 2,000km for unassisted take-off, and an overload condition of 4,000kg giving a 1,900km range with assisted take-off. For the series, with the FHL 131/Z as tail arma-

ment, the design flying weight was 28,000kg. The powerplant was to be six BMW 003 A-1 turbines, but it was possible to use Jumo 004 B-1s or 004 C-1s without major modification.

The airframe of the Ju 287 V 1 was a converted He 177 A-3 fuselage with the tail and rudder from the Ju 188 G-2 and a fixed main and nose undercarriage from an American B-24 Liberator. One Jumo 004 B-1 engine was mounted on either side of the forward fuselage, and another engine under each wing. The first flight of the Ju 287 V 1 took place on 8 August 1944. The Ju 287 V 2 was virtually identical to the V 1, but its elevators were 0.3m larger. In

Left: A collection of aerodynamic models for the Junkers development aircraft (EF) 116, which were tested in the Dessau wind tunnel.

Left: The Ju EF 122 was the forerunner of the first heavy jet bomber in the world, the Ju 287. Wind tunnel tests were carried out in October 1944.

addition to the two fuselage-mounted Jumo 004 engines, this aircraft had four BMW 003 turbines in pairs under the wings. Conversion to a layout with three engines under each wing, without the fuselage-mounted engines, was also envisaged.

Despite the serious situation prevailing by that time, it was still intended to build 75 Ju 287s up to July 1945. The order was, however, described as 'uncertain'.

On 16 April 1945 Allied troops reached Fliegerhorst Brandis, where two days previously the majority of the available aircraft and test models of the Luftwaffe had been blown up.

The airframe of the Ju 287 V 3 was to have been built from new. It was to have two groups of three BMW 003 A-1 turbojets under the wings. This aircraft was used as the basis for the EF 131, which was assembled after the war at the order of the Soviet Union. The EF 131 V 1 was cleared for flight in the summer of 1946 at Dessau, and in the autumn was dismantled and transferred to the Moscow region, where flight tests took place in the early summer of 1947.

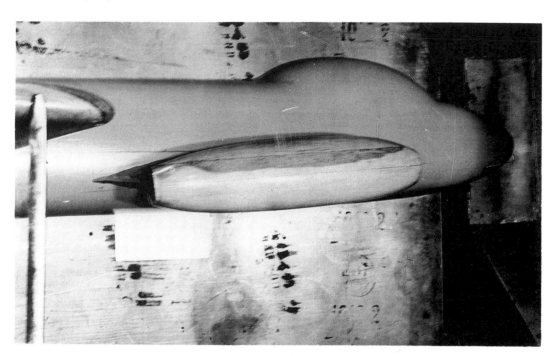

Right: Wind tunnel testing of the model of the Ju EF 122 C was concluded on 22 July 1944.

Right: The Ju 287 V 1 was powered by four Jumo 004 B-1 turbojets, with three rockets for assisted take-offs.

Left: The proposed mass production model of the Ju 287, with four HeS 11 jet engines.

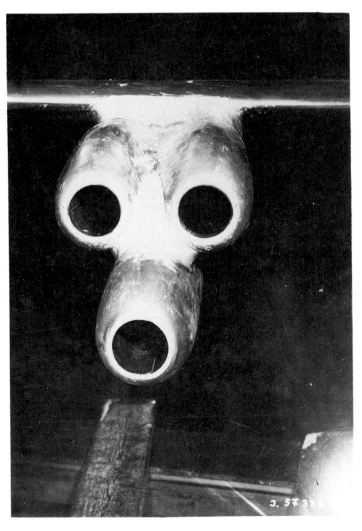

Below left: Because of the lack of sufficient high-powered engines, it was planned to group existing engines together — three BMW 003s are shown.

Below: The Ju EF 131 was built from parts of the Ju 287. Four were produced under Soviet direction, and at least one was flight-tested.